RIDING MACHINES
For Kids

RIDING MACHINES
For Kids

A Family Workshop Book
By Ed & Stevie Baldwin

CHILTON BOOK COMPANY
Radnor, Pennsylvania

Copyright ©1984 by The Family Workshop
Published in Radnor, Pa. by Chilton Book Company
Library of Congress Catalog Card Number: 83-43300
ISBN: 0-8019-7506-9
Manufactured in the United States of America

Created by The Family Workshop, Inc.
Managing Editor: F. Van Huntley
Editorial Director: Janet Weberling
Editors: Rhonda Mulberry, Mike McUsic, Rob Dickerson
Art Director: Dale Crain
Assistant Art Director: Christopher Berg
Production Artists: Roberta Taff, Wanda Young, Janice Harris Burstall,
                   Verna Stonecipher-Fuller
Typography: Deborah Gahm
Creative Director: April Bail
Workshop Director: D. J. Olin
Photography: Bill Welch
Project Designs: Ed and Stevie Baldwin, D. J. Olin, April Bail

1 2 3 4 5 6 7 8 9 0   3 2 1 0 9 8 7 6 5 4

This book is dedicated to Lou Olin, an honorary member of The Family, for her support, inspiration, and the ever present smile on D.J.'s face.

Preface

Producing this book has been fun. All concerned let their imaginations run wild in conceiving, designing, and building the riding machines featured in this book. As you will see, some of us were nostalgic and came up with a number of rocking toys. Others looked ahead and promoted the spaceship and other futuristic designs. We are very pleased with the final selection of riding machines included: They are easy to build and our kids are having great fun with them. We hope that you will find them just as attractive.

The book begins with a section on tips and techniques for buying and working with wood. We strongly recommend that you read this section before beginning any of the projects. It provides basic information on materials, tools, and terminology for the beginner and might just teach the old pro a new trick.

Each project plan contains a list of required materials and provides thoroughly illustrated step-by-step instructions for building that particular riding machine. Almost all projects can be built using common hand and/or hand-held power tools.

We would like to offer special thanks to a number of companies who provided materials, tools or services for building the projects. Tools supplied by Black & Decker and Shopsmith performed superbly. The stain, which produced such a fine finish on some of the projects was provided by Watco-Dennis Corporation. Last, but not least, we would like to thank the Frank Paxton Lumber Company for providing lumber.

Our children and those of many of our friends are now daily enjoying the riding toys we produced for this book. Thus far, the only mishap occured when a certain young lad attempted to plow his mother's flower garden with the tractor. Fortunately, the only damage was to the marigolds and, subsequently, to the youngster's derriere. We do seriously suggest that you provide some basic safety instructions to the lucky child receiving a riding machine, especially if he or she will be navigating on sidewalks or streets.

We trust that the riding machines you build will be enjoyed and appreciated as ours have been.

Contents

Tips & Techniques

Every toymaker with a bit of elfin talent has his or her own tried-and-true techniques for the shaping of wood into a finished toy. This is not an attempt to persuade you away from the way you do things best, but is intended to provide some essential information concerning the materials, terms, and techniques that we used for the projects in this book. Some of the information may be old hat to you – some may be new – and some you may disagree with. If there's one thing we know for certain about elves, it's that we all approach the art of working with wood a bit differently.

Included here you'll find discussions of various types of lumber, preservatives and finishes, adhesives, fasteners, joints, and some miscellanea that will be helpful in using this book. We suggest that you read the Tips & Techniques all the way through, or at least scan them, before you begin work on any project.

WOODWORKING TIPS
Selecting Wood

Different types of wood often have vastly different characteristics. This makes certain woods better for specific purposes than others. In addition, lumber is graded according to quality. We'll talk about types of wood first, then we'll discuss the grading system.

Woods are divided into two general categories: hard and soft. Most hardwoods are much more difficult to cut and work with, but usually are more sturdy and long-lived than softwoods. Softwoods are a lot easier to work with. The most commonly available softwoods are fir, redwood, hemlock, cedar, cypress, larch, spruce, and pine. Douglas is a particularly good fir; pine usually is available in both white (finer grain) and yellow (coarser grain).

Softwoods vary widely in their tendency to shrink, swell, and warp. Those least likely to do so are redwood, white pine, spruce, cedar, and cypress. Of these, cypress is more difficult to work with than the others and spruce is less decay resistant. Part of what makes a board more or less rot resistant is the portion of the tree from which it is cut. **Figure A** illustrates the difference between a heartwood board and one that is cut farther from the center of the tree. The more densely-packed annual rings near the center of the tree produce a highly rot resistant board, while boards cut from farther out may offer very little resistance, even when the stock is redwood or cedar. At the lumberyard, examine the ends of the boards carefully. The pattern of and distance between rings will tell you a lot about how long your children's riding toys will last.

Lumber is graded, as we mentioned earlier. We have provided a rundown of the grading system for pine, which is also used for most other types of lumber. Keep firmly in mind that you need not use the highest grade of lumber for every (or any) project. If you are in doubt as to which grade to use for a specific project, talk it over with your lumber dealer. Show him the plans so he gets the whole picture.

Figure A

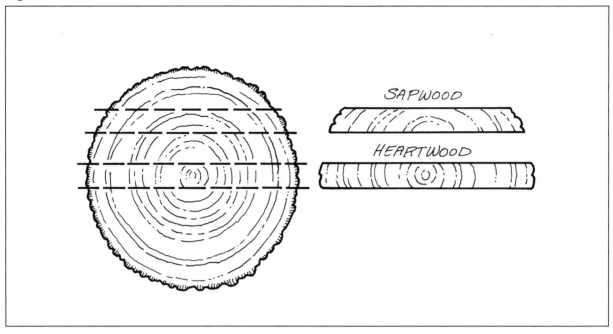

#5 common – Full of knots, knotholes, and other headaches but the least expensive, this grade of lumber should be used only when structural strength is not required and when you intend to paint. It is prone to check (crack along the grain), and usually will not be as thoroughly seasoned or dried as the higher grades.

#4 common – This grade is low in cost and has lots of imperfections, but less so than #5. It is good for projects in which appearance is not crucial.

#3 common – Small knotholes are common and knots are sometimes easily dislodged while you work. This is a better grade than #4 or #5, but is still prone to check.

#2 common – This grade should be free of knotholes but still has its share of knots.

#1 common – This is the top quality of the regular board grades. It may have small knots and other insignificant imperfections but should have no knotholes and is a good choice for projects in which small defects are not important.

D select – This is the lowest quality of the better-grade boards.

C select – This grade may have a few small blemishes on one side, but should be almost perfect on the other. It is usually used for indoor work only.

#1 and #2 clear – These are the best and most expensive grades. Spend the money if you wish to, but don't waste it! Use these grades only for the finest indoor and outdoor projects.

In addition to being graded by quality, wood stock will be more or less "wet." Wetness refers to the amount of sap still left in the wood when you buy it. Newly cut lumber is quite wet and must be air or kiln dried (seasoned) before it can be used. There is always some sap left, but it should be a very small amount. Wood that is not sufficiently dry will warp, crack, and shrink much more than dried wood. Unfortunately, there is no sure way to assess the amount of sap still left in the wood, even though the dealer may assure you it has been kiln dried. About the only hint we can give is to look at the end grain of each board (see **Figure A** again). Heartwood that is not sufficiently dry will become thinner as it loses moisture but is less likely to warp than sapwood.

When using lower grades of lumber, and consequently saving your bankroll, use your head as well.

Buy a little extra so that you can eliminate the worst knots and cracks. You can repair the lumber by filling small cracks and gouges using wood putty or a mixture of glue and sawdust. Warped boards sometimes can be weighted and straightened, but be aware that this takes time. Tap all knots to see which ones will fall out, and then glue them back in place. If a board is badly checked at the ends it's best to cut off the cracked portion, because exposure to the elements will worsen the cracks and perhaps even split the entire board. Minor checking should be filled as for cracks and gouges.

Finishes

PLEASE NOTE that no wooden toy should be left outdoors or otherwise exposed to the elements for any length of time no matter how it is finished. The projects presented in this book should last generations if properly cared for.

For final finishing and sealing of wooden riding toys you may wish to paint some of the projects you make, but if you use any of the more attractive woods it seems a shame to cover the natural grain and color. If you do paint be certain to select a non-toxic paint. Small children will chew on anything and believe it or not, wood doesn't taste half-bad.

Adhesive

We recommend both glue and fasteners (either nails, screws, or bolts) for all joints, unless you want to be able to disassemble the project for easy storage or transport. As an additional defense against the elements, you'll need a waterproof glue. Be forewarned that the term is sometimes used loosely on product labels. We suggest that you use a marine glue or a two-part epoxy that must be mixed and used immediately. Waterproof glue also may be brushed on like paint to seal end grain and prohibit water absorption. As a general rule, all glue assemblies should be clamped, but not so tightly as to force out most of the glue. Thirty minutes is sufficient clamping time for most joints. Those that will be under a great deal of stress should be clamped overnight. Joints secured with power-driven screws need not be clamped at all.

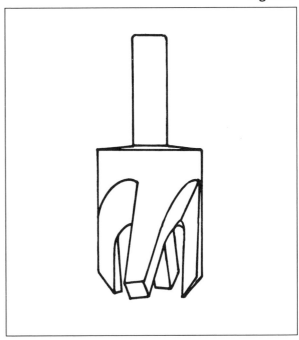

Fasteners and Other Hardware

Under normal conditions, ordinary hardware will suffice. However, if you suspect that the riding toys will be exposed to the elements, you may wish to use hardware which is not subject to rust. Galvanized hardware is more rustproof, but better yet are fasteners made of brass, bronze, and alloyed stainless steel. If you can't find galvanized hardware, or don't wish to pay more for brass, bronze, or stainless, look for a rust-inhibiting product with which to coat steel hardware.

Screws should always be countersunk. This will prevent the possibility of little ones sustaining scratches caused by slightly protruding screw heads. In the same vein, finishing nails may be recessed but common nails usually are not. If you countersink the screws, the recesses may be filled with wooden plugs or wood filler. Wooden plugs will be almost invisible if you cut them from stock that matches the grain of the surrounding wood. This is easy to do, using a plug cutter (**Figure B**). Plugs also can be made by cutting slices from dowel rod, but they present end grain and will be much more apparent, particularly if the wood is stained.

Figure C

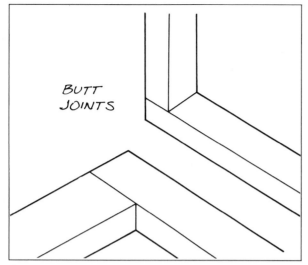

Figure D

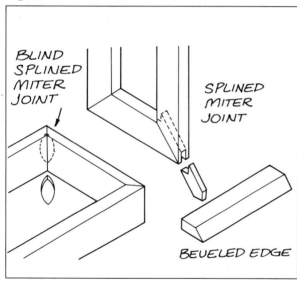

Figure E

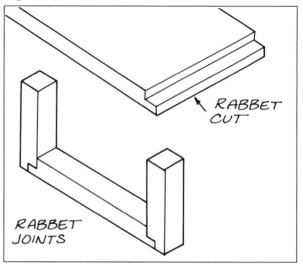

Cutting and Joining

Butt Joints: A butt joint normally connects the end of one piece to the surface or edge of another (**Figure C**). The end grain of one piece will always show. Because there are no cuts made to form interlocking portions, this is an extemely weak joint. A butt joint can be strengthened using glue blocks, splines, nails, screws, dowels, or other reinforcement.

Miters and Bevels: A miter joint connects two angle-cut ends (**Figure D**). It conceals the end grain of both pieces and can be reinforced using splines, dowels, or fasteners. The most common miter is a 45-degree, which is used to construct right-angle assemblies. A bevel is an angle cut made along an edge or surface.

Rabbets: A rabbet is an L-shaped groove and has many applications. A rabbet cut into one or both pieces to be joined conceals the end grain of one piece and allows for a greater surface area to be glued, thus creating a stronger joint (**Figure E**). Normally it is reinforced using screws or nails.

Dado: Basically, a dado is a groove. Several types of dadoes and dado joints are illustrated in **Figure F**. A through dado extends all the way from edge to edge (or end to end). A stopped dado extends from one edge to a point short of the opposite edge. A blind dado is stopped short of both edges.

Lap Joints: A lap joint normally is used to connect two members at right angles. In the most common lap joint, the two joined surfaces are flush (**Figure G**). This joint provides a large area to be glued.

Mortise and Tenon Joints: There are lots of variations on this theme, but the basic garden-variety mortise and tenon joints are shown in **Figure H**. This is an extremely strong joint and can be made even stronger. A pegged (or pinned) mortise and tenon joint is one in

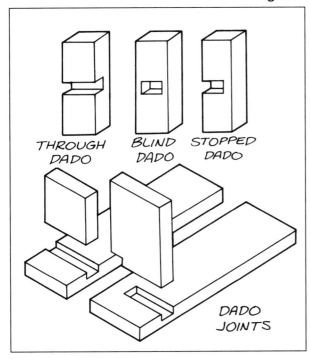

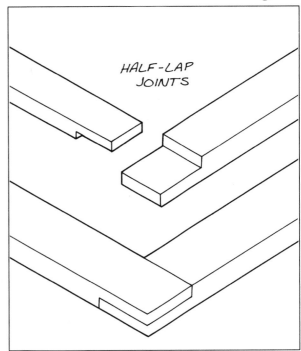

which the tenon extends out beyond the mortise and is itself mortised to accommodate a peg. The unglued, pegged mortise and tenon is a handy joint to use in projects that you wish to disassemble for portability.

Spline Joints: A spline is a thin strip of wood used as a connecting member between two boards. It fits into dadoes cut into the edges to be joined, and can be used to strengthen any type of joint. A spline joint is shown in **Figure I**. Through splines reach from end to end. Blind splines are stopped short of the ends and cannot be seen once the joint is assembled.

Splines are specified in this book to create large parts that require several edge-joined boards to achieve an indicated width. A splined-edge joint is much stronger than one which is simply glued and clamped. Unglued splines create a structure that can expand and contract with atmospheric conditions without cracking or splitting. Unglued splines can be used, of course, only for parts that are secured at the ends to trim or other structures. In the boards that are splined together to form a wall, for instance, the splines usually may be left un-

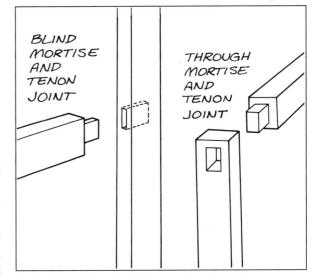

glued since the wall is attached on all four edges to other structures. When edge-joining, every other board should be turned so that the ray patterns are alternated (**Figure J**) to avoid warping.

Figure I

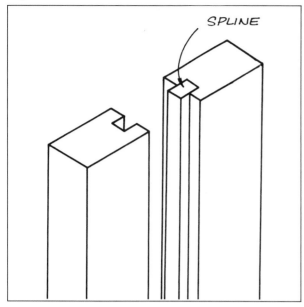

SPLINE

Figure J

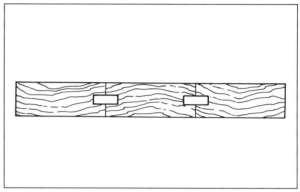

Figure K

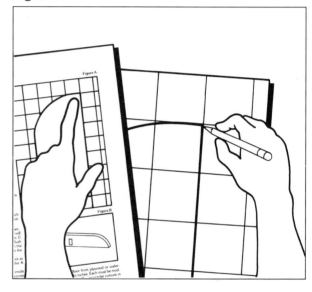

Waste Allowance

We have specified the materials required to build each project in this book. Because you cannot use every single inch of stock, especially if you purchase a lower grade of wood, we have added a waste allowance of approximately ten percent to each material called for. Special instances in which a waste allowance is not included are noted. Although it may sound like a fairly large amount, ten percent is not really a lot to allow for waste. Keep this in mind when you are at the lumberyard. We suggest that you initially purchase only enough stock to make one project, and note how much extra you have after all the parts are cut. This will give you a better basis on which to judge your purchases for subsequent projects.

Enlarging Scale Drawings

For unusually shaped or contoured parts, whenever possible we have provided full-size patterns or cutting diagrams that can be plotted directly on the wood using basic tools such as a square and angle measure. In some instances, however, we had to provide scale drawings, which are shown on a background grid of squares. Each small square on the grid is equal to a 1-inch square on the full-size part, and the drawing must be enlarged to make a full-size pattern. To enlarge a scale drawing you'll need a large piece of paper containing a grid of 1-inch squares. You can make your own pattern paper by drawing the 1-inch grid on brown wrapping paper, shelf paper, or flattened grocery bags, or you can purchase pattern paper that already contains the grid. It is available in at least two forms: as draft paper (check an art supply store) and as dressmaker's pattern paper. To enlarge the scale drawing simply reproduce the lines onto the paper containing the larger grid, working one square at a time (**Figure K**).

Dump Truck

The only thing missing from this fully functional dump truck is a membership in the Teamster's Union. It is pedal powered, has working steering, a fold down windshield, an imaginary engine compartment, tool storage under the seat, and last but not least a working dump bed! This little ten-wheeler is a guaranteed winner with any young truck driver.

Figure A

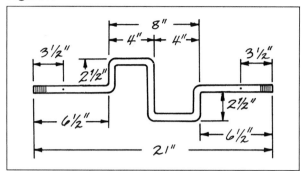

Materials

25 square feet of ¾-inch pine. We used standard 1 x 12 lumber.

28 square feet of ¼-inch-thick plywood, with both sides finished.

30-inch length of standard pine 2 x 4.

Wooden dowel rod: 1-foot-length of ⅜-inch, 12 feet of ½-inch, 18-inch length of ¾-inch, 2-foot length of 1-inch, and a 2-inch length of 1½-inch. For the optional "flip-top" hood ornament, you'll need a 1-inch length of ⅛-inch-diameter dowel rod, or you can use a toothpick.

One eyescrew, approximately ⅜ inch in diameter.

Six eyescrews, approximately ½ inch in diameter.

Three piano hinges, each 11¾ inches long, and two 12½ inches long, each with screws to fit.

Two flush hinges, each 1¾ inches long, each with screws to fit.

Two metal conduit clamps that will accommodate ½-inch-diameter pipe.

Metal axle rods: two straight rods for the front and rear axles, each ½ inch in diameter and 21 inches long; and one rod for the "drive" axle, ½ inch in diameter and 33 inches long, threaded on both ends and bent as shown in **Figure A**. If you're not confident about bending this rod yourself, ask for help at a hardware store, metal shop, or service station. Each of the straight axle rods will need to be drilled through, ¼ inch from each end, to accommodate the cotter pins that hold the wheels in place. The bent drive axle will also need to be drilled through to accommodate cotter pins, 3½ inches from each end.

Two locknuts to fit the ends of the drive axle.

Six cotter pins.

Twelve metal washers, each with a ⅝-inch center hole.

Ten machine bolts: one bolt 4½ inches long, ⅜ inch in diameter, with two flat washers, one spring lock washer, and a nut to fit; one bolt 3½ inches long, ¼ inch in diameter, with three flat washers, and a nut to fit; four bolts, each 2 inches long and ¼ inch in diameter, each with three flat washers and a nut to fit; and four bolts, each 2½ inches long and ¼ inch in diameter, each with two flat washers and a nut to fit.

Two sheet metal screws, each ¾ inch long, with washers to fit.

Ten wheels, each 8 inches in diameter and 1¾ inches wide. We used lawn mower wheels.

6-foot length of ⅛-inch-diameter plastic-covered cable.

Finishing nails, No. 6 gauge flathead wood screws, carpenter's wood glue, wood filler, non-toxic paint in your choice of colors, and pattern paper or drafting paper with a grid of 1-inch squares (see the Tips & Techniques section of this book).

Building the Frame

The assembled frame is shown in **Figure B**. Refer to this diagram as you work through this section.

1. A scale drawing of the frame Rail is provided in **Figure C**. Enlarge the drawing to make a full-size paper pattern, and cut two Rails from ¾-inch pine. It's important that the two Rails be identical, so the axles holes will line up properly. To accomplish this we suggest that you begin by cutting two 9 x 59-inch rectangles from ¾-inch pine, nail them together temporarily, and cut the pieces simultaneously. Drill a ½-inch-diameter axle hole through both pieces, centered 7½ inches from the upper edge of the axle extension.

2. Each Rail is reinforced by plywood Facings which are cut to match the rear portion (**Figure D**). Cut four pieces of plywood, each 9 x 19 inches, and nail them together temporarily. Use the rear portion of one wooden Rail as a pattern to cut the plywood Facings and drill the axle holes.

3. Glue and nail a plywood Facing to each side of one Rail (**Figure D**). Attach the remaining Facings to the other Rail.

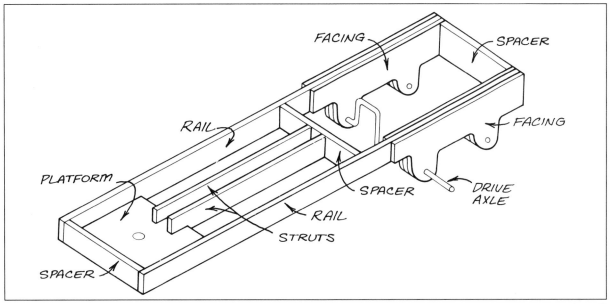

FACING

SPACER

FACING

RAIL

PLATFORM

SPACER

DRIVE AXLE

RAIL

STRUTS

SPACER

Figure C

1 square = 1 inch

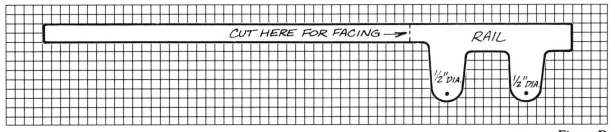

CUT HERE FOR FACING →

RAIL

½" DIA.   ½" DIA.

4. Three spacers serve to connect the two Rails. Cut three Spacers from ¾-inch pine: two 2 x 10½ inches, and one 3 x 10 inches.

5. Align the two Rails and insert one end of the bent drive axle into the front hole in each one. Glue the 3-inch-wide Spacer between the Rails flush with the back ends as shown in **Figure B**. Glue one of the remaining Spacers between the Frame pieces, flush with the front ends. Insert the third Spacer between the Frame pieces 35¼ inches from the front end. Secure the Spacers with screws.

6. A Platform is attached between the Rails at the front. It serves to support the front end of the steering assembly, and the front axle is suspended from it. Cut one Platform, 7½ x 10½ inches, from ¾-inch pine. In

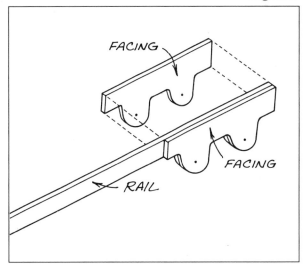

FACING

FACING

RAIL

DUMP TRUCK

9

Figure E

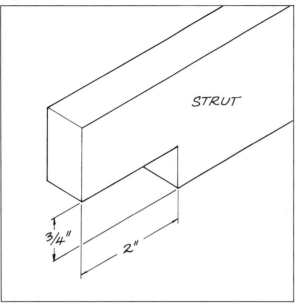

STRUT

3/4"

2"

addition, cut two Braces from the same material, each 1¼ x 7½ inches. Drill a ½-inch-diameter hole through the Platform 1¼ inches from one long edge and centered between the sides. This hole will accommodate the machine bolt that supports the axle assembly.

7. Glue the Platform between the two Rails flush against the front Spacer, placing the bolt hole toward the rear (**Figure B**). The bottom of the platform should be flush with the lower edges of the Rails. Glue the Braces on top of the Platform, flush against the front Spacer and the Rails. Secure these joints with screws.

8. Two Struts are attached to the frame to support the pedal assemblies. Cut two Struts from ¾-inch pine, each 2 x 29 inches. Cut a ¾ x 2-inch notch in one end of each Strut, as shown in **Figure E**. Place the Struts between the middle Spacer and the back edge of the Platform (**Figure B**), centered between the two Rails and allowing a 1½-inch space between them. Temporarily secure both ends with screws.

Figure F

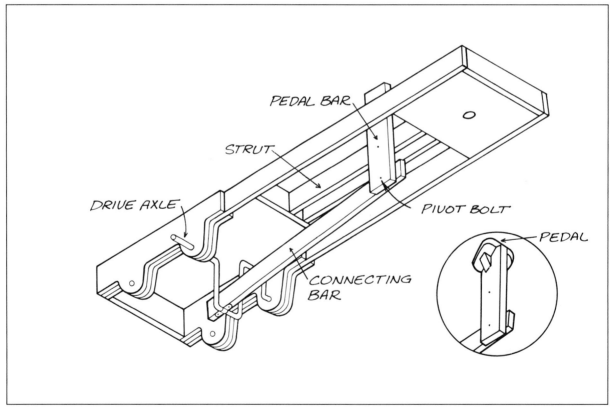

PEDAL BAR

STRUT

DRIVE AXLE

PIVOT BOLT

PEDAL

CONNECTING BAR

Rear Axles and Pedal Assembly

A diagram of the assembled pedal mechanism is provided in **Figure F**.

1. The bent drive axle is already in place. This is the only one of the three axles that will rotate. (The other two axles are stationary; the wheels rotate around them.) For this reason, the wheels on the drive axle must be secured tightly so they spin as the axle does. Perform the following procedures at each end of the drive axle. First, insert a cotter pin through the hole that was drilled 3½ inches from the end. Add a washer, two wheels, and another washer. Install a locknut and tighten it until the wheels are securely wedged against the inner washer and cotter pin.

2. Insert a straight axle through the rear holes, leaving equal extensions on each side. At each end, install a washer, two wheels, another washer, and a cotter pin.

3. Cut the following pieces from ¾-inch pine for the pedal mechanism: two Connecting Bars, each 2 x 28 inches; two Pedal Bars, each 2 x 14 inches; and two Pedals, each 3 x 4 inches. Round off each of the corners of the Pedals.

4. The Connecting Bars are attached to the drive axle at one end, and to the Pedal Bars at the opposite end. To attach one Connecting Bar to the drive axle, attach one flange of a metal conduit clamp on the narrow edge of the Bar, 1 inch from one end, as shown in **Figure G**. Place the Bar over one throw of the axle and slip the clamp over the axle as shown. Install the remaining clamp flange on the Bar. Attach the other Connecting Bar to the opposite throw of the drive axle in the same manner.

5. A hole drilled through the Bar near the opposite end will accommodate the pivot bolt that joins the Connecting Bar to the Pedal Bar. Drill a ⅜-inch-diameter hole through the Bar, 1½ inches from the front end.

6. Drill two ⅜-inch-diameter holes through each Pedal Bar: one 1½ inches from one short end, and one 6 inches from the first hole, measuring center to center (**Figure H**).

7. Join one of the Pedal Bars to the outer side of each Connecting Bar in the following manner. First, slip a washer over the end of a 2-inch-long bolt. Insert the bolt through the hole near the end of the Pedal Bar,

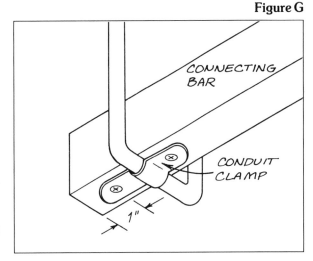

Figure G

CONNECTING BAR

CONDUIT CLAMP

1"

then add another washer. Insert the bolt through the hole near the front of the Connecting Bar, add another washer, and install the nut. Be sure to leave this assembly loose enough to rotate.

8. Rotate the axle until until the back end of one Connecting Bar is at the very bottom of its rotation cycle. The other Connecting Bar will now be at the top of its cycle. Chock the wheels so the axle will not turn as you work. At the front end of the Connecting Bar that is at the bottom of its cycle, move the Pedal Bar to a vertical position. Place the Pedal Bar against the outer side of the truck frame Strut (**Figure F**) and adjust it up or down until the open hole in the Pedal Bar is midway between the top and bottom edges of the Strut. (Make sure the Bar is still in a vertical position.) Mark the position of the hole on the Strut and drill a ⅜-inch-diameter hole through the Strut at this point. Slip a washer over the end of a 2-inch-long bolt and insert the bolt through the Pedal Bar. Add another washer, insert the bolt through the Strut, add a third washer, and install the nut, leaving the assembly loose enough to pivot.

9. Rotate the drive axle one-half turn, so that the free Connecting Bar is at the bottom of its cycle, and repeat the procedures in step 8 to join the remaining Pedal Bar and Strut. Note: it may be necessary to trim the tops of the Pedal Bars to make them a more comfortable length for your child. The Pedals, therefore, will be attached after you have built the cab, and can "fit" the Pedal Bars to the pint-sized driver.

Figure H

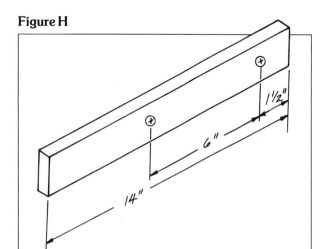

Building the Cab

The cab consists of plywood sides and the seat and hood assemblies.

1. We suggest that you cut the Cab Sides simultaneously, as you did the frame Rails. A scale drawing of the Cab Side is provided in **Figure I**. Enlarge the drawing to make a full size paper pattern and cut the two Cab

Sides from plywood. In addition, cut one Hood from the same material, 12½ x 13¼ inches.

2. Cut one Seat Back from ¾-inch pine, 13 x 12 inches. Since this piece is probably wider than your stock, it will be necessary to spline (or simply edge glue and clamp) two pieces together to create the Seat Back.

3. Begin the cab assembly by gluing the Cab Sides to the outer sides of the Rails, with front and lower edges flush. Secure the Sides with screws.

4. Insert and glue the Seat Back between the Cab Sides so that it rests on the middle Spacer and is flush with the back edges of the Cab Sides. Secure it with finishing nails driven through the Cab Sides.

5. Glue and nail the Hood over the edges of the Cab Sides as shown in **Figure J**. The Hood should not reach all the way to the front, but should be flush with the vertical edges of the Sides at the "dashboard" end.

6. To complete the seat assembly cut the following pieces from ¾-inch pine: one Seat, 7½ x 11⅞ inches; one Seat Front, 4¼ x 12 inches; and one Floor, 6½ x 11⅞ inches.

7. Glue and nail the Seat Front and Floor between the Cab Sides. The Seat Front should rest on the frame and line up flush with the vertical edges of the Sides at

Figure I   **1 square = 1 inch**

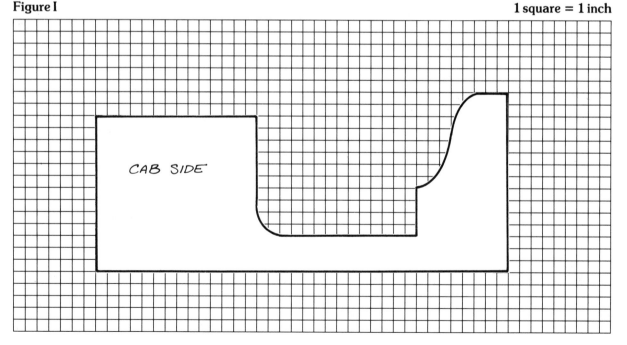

CAB SIDE

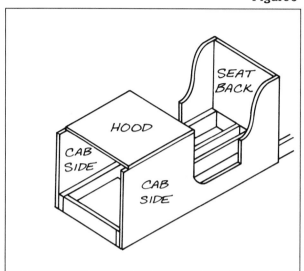

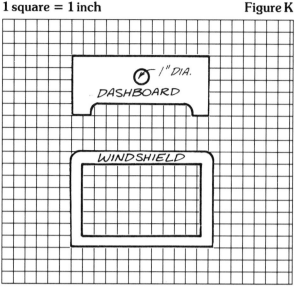

Figure L

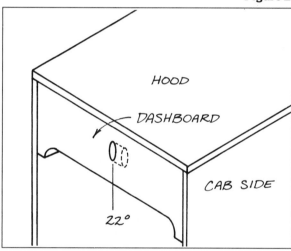

the front of the "seat" portion. The Floor should be flush with the lower edges of the frame assembly. Round off the corners of the Seat piece and place it between the Cab Sides so that it rests on top of the Seat Front and is flush against the Seat Back. Attach it to the Seat Back using an 11¾-inch piano hinge (**Figure M**).

8. The front portion of the cab consists of the Hood (which is already in place), the Dashboard, the Windshield, and the front grill assembly. Scale drawings for the Dashboard and the Windshield are provided in **Figure K**. Enlarge the drawings to make full-size paper patterns and cut one of each piece from ¾-inch pine. The hole that is shown in the Dashboard will accommodate the Steering Column, and should be drilled at a downward angle as shown in **Figure L**.

9. Glue and nail the Dashboard between the Cab Sides underneath the Hood. It should be flush with the rear edge of the Hood and the vertical edges of the Sides (**Figure L**).

10. Cut two Hood Supports, each 3 x 12 inches, from the ¾-inch pine. Glue and nail one Support underneath the Hood, placing one long edge flush against the Dashboard. Attach the other Support under the Hood, placing one long edge flush with the front edge of the Hood. Secure the Supports with nails driven through the Cab Sides.

11. Stand the Windshield in an upright position on top of the Hood, flush with the "dashboard" edge (**Figure M**). Attach it to the Hood using one of the remaining piano hinges.

12. The grill assembly (**Figure N**) consists of a four-sided frame and twelve grill rods. Cut the following frame pieces from ¾-inch pine: one Top, 1 x 12½ inches; one Bottom, 1 x 12 inches; and two Sides, each 1 x 9¼ inches. Cut twelve Grill Rods from ½-inch dowel, each 10½ inches long.

Figure M

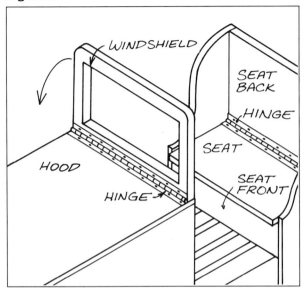

Figure N

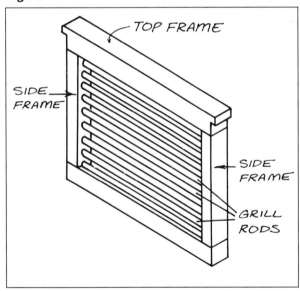

Figure O

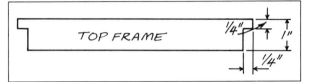

Figure P

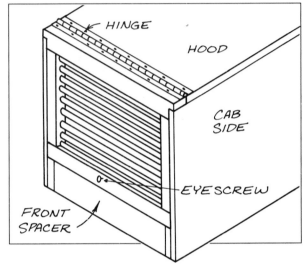

13. Drill twelve sockets into one long edge on each Side Frame to accommodate the rods. The sockets should be ½ inch in diameter and ¼ inch deep. Drill the first socket ½ inch from the end of the piece and space the subsequent sockets ¾ inch apart, measuring from center to center. The last socket should be ½ inch from the opposite end of the piece.

14. The Top Frame piece is notched on both ends to fit between the Cab Sides, as shown in **Figure O**. Cut the notches and then assemble the grill, butting the frame pieces as shown in **Figure N**.

15. Insert the grill between the Cab Sides at the front of the truck. The notched ends of the Top Frame piece should rest on top of the Cab Sides so that the grill is flush with the front edges. Attach the Top Frame piece to the Hood using one of the remaining piano hinge (**Figure P**). We installed the small eyescrew on the front of the Bottom Frame piece, to serve as a handle when lifting the grill.

16. Now you can "fit" the Pedal Bars to the dump-truck driver. The Pedals will be attached to the Pedal Bars as shown in **Figure F**. Cut off the top of the Pedal Bars, if necessary, to make them a more comfortable length. Then trim the back upper corner of each Bar to accommodate the Pedal. Glue a Pedal to each Bar and secure the joints with screws. Cut four small triangular glue blocks and use them to strengthen the Pedal-to-Pedal Bar joints.

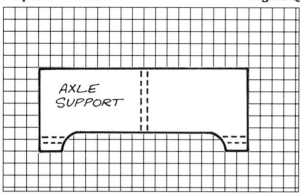

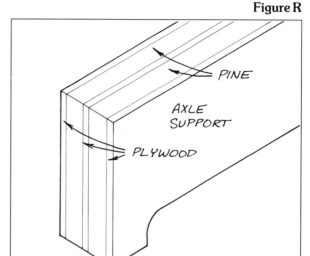

Building the Front Axle Assembly

1. The front axle support assembly is made by laminating alternating layers of pine and plywood. A scale drawing of the Axle Support is provided in **Figure Q**. Enlarge the drawing to make a full-sized paper pattern and cut five Axle Support pieces; two from ¾-inch pine and three from plywood.

2. Stack and glue the five Axle Support pieces as shown in **Figure R**. Clamp this assembly while the glue is allowed to dry.

3. Three holes are drilled through the Axle Support assembly: one from top to bottom to accommodate the machine bolt, and one through each of the lower extensions to accommodate the front axle (**Figure S**). Drill a ½-inch-diameter axle hole from end to end through the center of each lower extension of the assembly, being careful to align them so the axle will fit. The ½-inch-diameter bolt hole should be drilled straight down through the center of the assembly.

4. Lubricate the 4½-inch-long machine bolt and insert it into the hole in the axle assembly, from bottom to top. Add a flat washer and then insert the end of the bolt up through the hole in the Platform that is attached to the truck frame. Add another flat washer and the spring lock washer. Install the nut, leaving it loose enough to allow the axle assembly to swivel.

5. Insert the metal axle through the axle holes in the support assembly, leaving equal extensions on each side. At each end install a washer, a wheel, and another washer. Secure the wheel by inserting a cotter pin through the hole near the end of the axle.

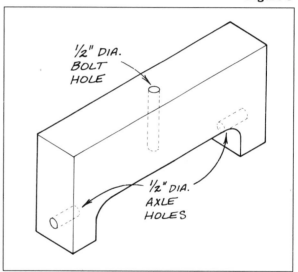

Steering Assembly

Steering is accomplished by means of a simple cord-and-pulley arrangement that connects the Steering Column to the front axle assembly (**Figure T**).

1. A 21-inch length of 1-inch-diameter wooden dowel rod serves as the Steering Column. Cut the Column and round off the edge at one end. This will be the lower end.

Figure T

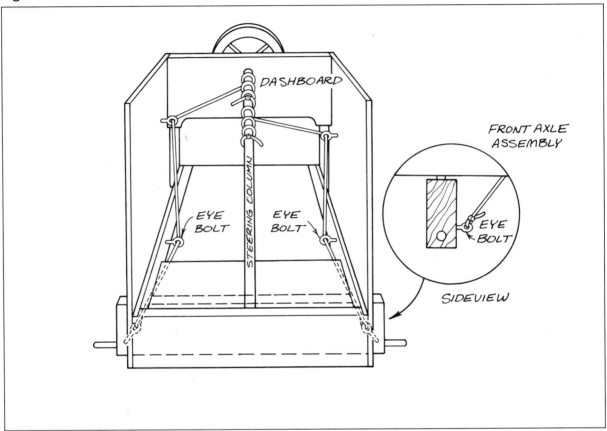

DASHBOARD

FRONT AXLE
ASSEMBLY

STEERING COLUMN

EYE
BOLT

EYE
BOLT

EYE
BOLT

SIDEVIEW

Figure U

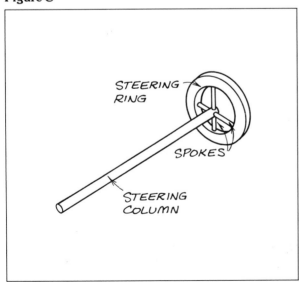

STEERING
RING

SPOKES

STEERING
COLUMN

2. The steering wheel assembly is attached to the upper end of the Column as shown in **Figure U**. The Steering Ring is a 7-inch-diameter circle cut from ¾-inch pine, with a 5-inch-diameter circle cut out of the center. A scale drawing for the Ring is provided in **Figure V**. Cut the Ring, and cut four 2½-inch-long Spokes from ⅜-inch-diameter wooden dowel rod.

3. Assemble the Steering Ring, Spokes, and Steering Column by drilling carefully aligned sockets into the Ring and Column to accommodate the ends of the Spokes. Glue the Spokes in place.

4. When the Steering Column is in place, the lower end is housed in a shallow socket to keep the Column steady. Insert the lower end of the Column through the hole in the Dashboard until it rests against the Platform and the front Spacer. Make sure the Column is straight,

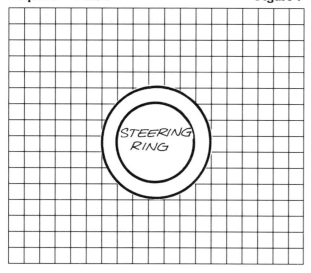

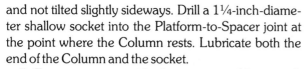

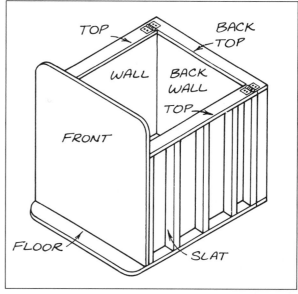

Figure X

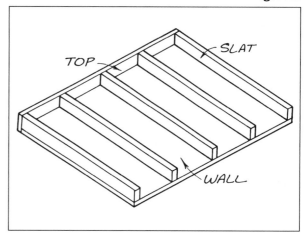

and not tilted slightly sideways. Drill a 1¼-inch-diameter shallow socket into the Platform-to-Spacer joint at the point where the Column rests. Lubricate both the end of the Column and the socket.

5. Two eyescrews guide the steering cable to each side of the axle support, as shown in **Figure T**. Install the eyebolts as shown in **Figure T**. Cut the plastic covered cable in half, so that you have two 3-foot lengths. Tie one end of each length to the eyescrew on each end of the axle support, as shown in **Figure T**. Thread each cable up through the eyescrew guides, as shown. Position the front wheels so that the dump truck rolls straight forward. Wrap the right-hand-wheel cable counter-clockwise around the Steering Column, starting near the upper end and working down, as shown. Pull the cable taut, and insert a screw with a flat washer over the end of the cable to secure it to the Steering Column as shown. Attach the left-hand-wheel cable to the Steering Column in the same manner, wrapping it clockwise.

Building the Dump Bed

The assembled dump bed is shown in **Figure W**. It is basically an open box made from plywood, with solid pine slats (for extra strength) and a hinged back.

1. Cut the following pieces from plywood for the dump bed sides: two Walls, each 15 x 20 inches; and two Tops, each 1¾ x 20 inches. Cut ten Slats from ¾-inch pine, each 1½ x 15 inches.

2. Assemble two identical sides (**Figure X**) using the pieces you cut in step 1. All joints should be glued and secured with finishing nails.

3. Cut the following pieces from plywood for the dump bed back: one Wall, 15 x 17 inches; and two Top/Bottom pieces, each 1¾ x 17 inches. Cut five Slats from ¾-inch pine, each 1½ x 15 inches. Assemble the back (**Figure Y**), glueing and nailing all joints.

Figure Y

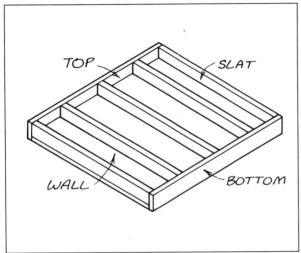

TOP — SLAT
WALL — BOTTOM

Figure Z

FLOOR
HINGE

4. Cut the following pieces from plywood to complete the dump bed: one Floor, 17 x 22 inches; and one Front, 17 x 17 inches. Round off two corners of the Floor at the ends of one short edge. (This will be the front edge.) Round off any two adjacent corners of the Front. (This will be the top edge.)

5. Glue one side assembly to the Floor as shown in **Figure W**. One end of the side assembly should be flush with the rear edge of the Floor. The opposite end will be about two inches from the front of the Floor. The outer edges of the Slats should be flush with the edge of the Floor. Glue the remaining side assembly to the Floor, flush with the opposite edge and positioned in the same manner. Secure the Floor and Side assemblies by driving nails or screws up through the Floor into the ends of the Slats.

6. Glue the plywood Front to the front ends of the side assemblies and to the Floor. Secure it with finishing nails or screws.

7. Place the assembled back against the ends of the side assemblies so that all edges are flush. Use the two short hinges to attach the back to each side assembly as shown in **Figure W**.

8. Use the remaining piano hinge to attach the assembled dump bed to the frame, so that the rear surfaces are flush (**Figure Z**).

Adding the Trim

The trim consists of fenders, running boards, lights, a front bumper, and a few other goodies (**Figure AA**). This section also includes instructions for making the lever that raises and lowers the dump bed.

1. Cut two Running Boards from ¾-inch pine, each 1 x 22 inches. On each side of the truck cab, glue one long edge of the Running Board to the Cab Side, placing lower and rear edges flush. Secure the Running Boards with screws. We rounded off the the back outside corner of each Running Board.

2. Enlarge the drawings in **Figure BB** to make full-size paper patterns and cut two Upper Fenders and Two Lower Fenders from ¾-inch pine. Bevel the rear edge of each Upper and Lower Fender, and the front edge of the Lower Fender, and glue them to the Cab Sides as shown in **Figure AA**. The bottom of the Lower Fender should rest on the Running Board. Secure the Fenders with screws inserted through the Cab Sides.

3. To make the Side Hood Ornaments, cut four 4-inch lengths of ¾-inch dowel rod and slice each rod in half lengthwise. Glue four of these pieces to each Cab Side as shown in **Figure AA**.

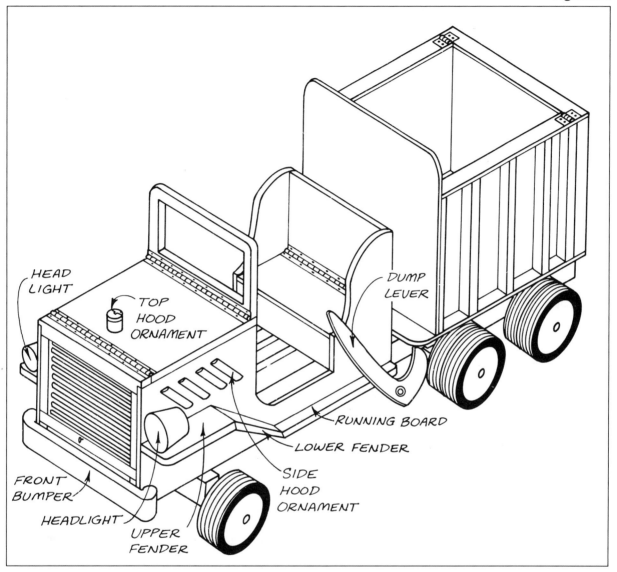

HEAD LIGHT

TOP HOOD ORNAMENT

DUMP LEVER

RUNNING BOARD

LOWER FENDER

SIDE HOOD ORNAMENT

FRONT BUMPER

HEADLIGHT

UPPER FENDER

4. The Top Hood Ornament is made from a short length of 1½-inch-diameter dowel rod. You can either glue it to the Hood as is, or go through a few more gyrations to create a "flip-top" ornament (**Figure CC**). To do this, cut a ¼-inch-thick slice from one end of the rod. Drill a ⅛-inch-diameter hole through the slice (**Figure DD**), and then cut the slice into three pieces as shown. Reassemble the three pieces into their original shape and insert a short length of ⅛-inch-diameter dowel rod through the aligned holes. Drill out the center length of the original piece of dowel rod, using a ⅞-inch-diameter bit, to create an empty cylinder shape. Glue the cylinder to the Hood near the front. Place the assembled "flip-top" on top of the cylinder and glue only the two small "hinge" pieces to the cylinder, leaving the larger piece free to open and close.

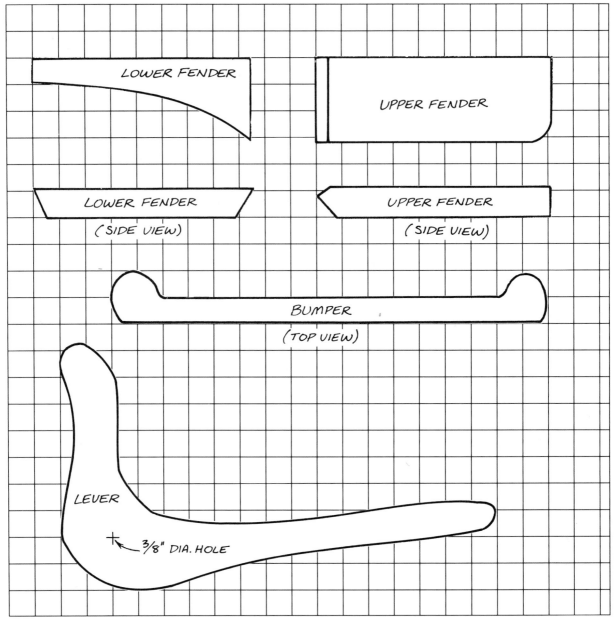

5. A scale drawing (top view) of the Front Bumper is provided in **Figure BB**. Enlarge the drawing to make a full-size paper pattern and cut one Bumper from pine 2 x 4.

6. The Bumper is connected to the front of the truck frame Spacer by means of two short dowel rods (**Figure EE**). Cut two 1½-inch-lengths of ½-inch-diameter dowel and drill shallow sockets into the Bumper and Spacer to accommodate the ends. Glue the assembly in place.

Figure CC   **Figure DD**

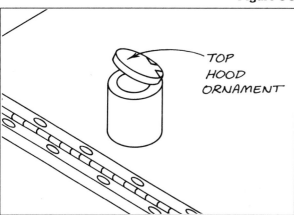

TOP
HOOD
ORNAMENT

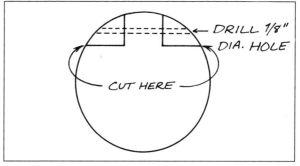

DRILL ⅛"
DIA. HOLE

CUT HERE

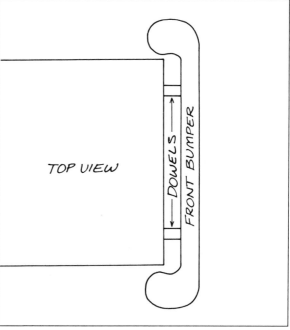

TOP VIEW

DOWELS

FRONT BUMPER

7. To make one Headlight, cut two 3-inch lengths from the pine 2 x 4. Glue them together to form a 3 x 3 x 3½-inch block. When the glue has cured, cut the block into a 2½-inch-diameter cylinder. If you have access to a lathe, you can turn the block to create a slightly tapered Headlight. Make another Headlight in the same manner, and glue one Headlight to each Fender as shown in **Figure AA**.

8. The Tail Lights are simple 1½-inch-diameter circles cut from plywood (or sliced dowel rod) and glued to the back of the truck frame as shown in **Figure FF**.

9. The dump bed is operated by means of a Lever attached to the side of the cab (**Figure AA**). A scale drawing for the Lever is provided in **Figure BB**. Enlarge the drawing to make a full-size paper pattern and cut one lever from ¾-inch pine. Drill a hole where indicated in the scale drawing.

10. Place the Lever against the Running Board on one side of the cab (**Figure AA**) so that the front end is accessible to the driver and the back end touches the bottom of the dump bed approximately 4½ inches from the front of the dump bed Floor. Mark the position of the hole in the Lever on the Running Board. Drill a ⅜-inch-diameter hole all the way through the Running Board, Cab Side, and Frame. Slip a washer over the end of the 3½-inch-long bolt and insert the bolt through the Lever. Add another washer, insert the bolt through the hole in the truck side, add a third washer, and secure with a nut. Leave the nut loose enough to allow the Lever to be moved up and down.

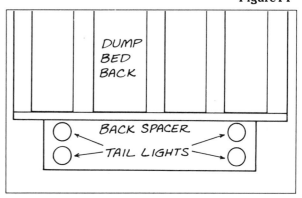

DUMP
BED
BACK

BACK SPACER

TAIL LIGHTS

Double-Duty Wagon

Luckily, this is a very easy project to build. We say "luckily" because you're probably going to end up making several: one for the kids; one for the family gardener; one for hauling the trash and the firewood. This is our only prototype that hasn't been "kid-tested;" the kids haven't had a chance to get near it yet. (It's MINE!)

Materials

Waferwood: 26 x 34-inch piece of ¾-inch, and a 12 x 12-inch piece of ¼-inch.

3 linear feet of 2 x 4 pine lumber.

2 linear feet of 2 x 8 pine lumber.

12 linear feet of 1 x 4 pine lumber.

4-foot length of 1-inch-diameter wooden dowel rod.

1-foot length of ¾-inch-diameter wooden dowel rod.

10-inch length of ¼-inch-diameter wooden dowel rod.

One ⅝-inch-diameter stove bolt, 2½ inches long, with a nut and 3 washers.

Nine ¾-inch, flathead wood screws; handful each of 2d, 3d, and 4d finishing nails; six 4d and four 8d common nails.

Carpenter's wood glue.

Beeswax or other lubricant.

Cutting the Parts

1. Cut these pieces from the ¾-inch waferwood:

Description	Dimensions	Quantity
Floor	16 x 24 inches	1
Sides	5 x 25½ inches	2
Ends	5 x 16 inches	2

Drill a ¾-inch-diameter hole through the Floor, 3 inches from one short end and centered between the long sides.

2. Cut one Hinge Support from ¾-inch waferwood using the scale drawing provided in **Figure A**.

3. Cut eight Washers from ¼-inch waferwood, each 3 inches in diameter. Drill a 1⅛-inch-diameter hole through the center of each.

4. Cut four Wheels from 2 x 8 lumber, each 6 inches in diameter. Drill a 1⅛-inch-diameter hole through the exact center of each.

5. Cut the following pieces from 1 x 4 lumber:

Description	Length	Quantity
Supports	4¼ inches	8
Side Rails	27½ inches	2
End Rails	19¼ inches	2

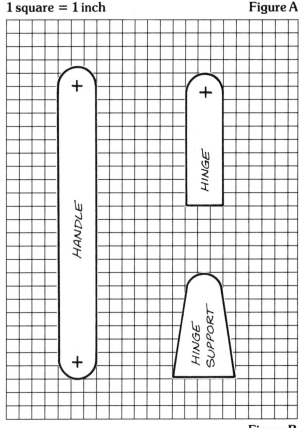

1 square = 1 inch   **Figure A**

HANDLE

HINGE

HINGE SUPPORT

Figure B

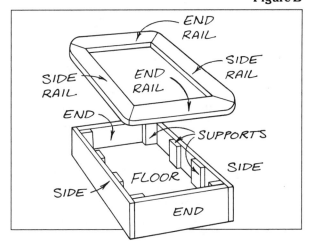

END RAIL

SIDE RAIL

SIDE RAIL

END RAIL

END

SIDE

SUPPORTS

SIDE

FLOOR

SIDE

END

The ends of the Side and End Rails are cut at a 45-degree angle to form a 27½ x 19¼-inch (outer dimensions) "frame" as shown in **Figure B**.

Figure C

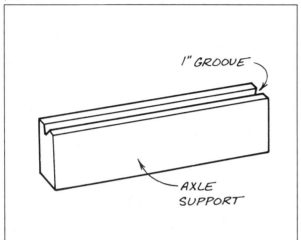

Figure E

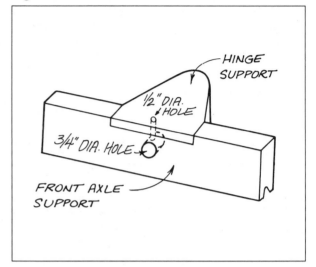

Figure D

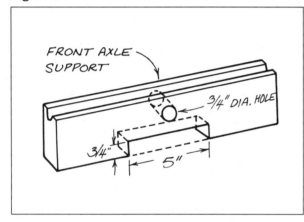

6. Cut one Handle and two Hinges from 1 x 4 lumber using the scale drawings provided in **Figure A**. Drill holes through these pieces according to the positions and sizes indicated on the scale drawings.

7. Cut two Axles, each 20 inches long, from the 1-inch-diameter wooden dowel rod. Drill a ¼-inch-diameter hole, 1½ inches from each end of each Axle.

8. Cut one Hinge Pin 5 inches long, and one Handle Bar 7 inches long, from ¾-inch-diameter wooden dowel rod.

9. Cut four Axle Pins, each 2½ inches long, from the ¼-inch-diameter wooden dowel rod.

10. Cut 2 Axle Supports, each 14 inches long, from 2 x 4 lumber.

Assembly

Once the sawdust has settled, the assembly of the wagon is as easy as 1, 2, 3 (literally).

One – The Wagon Box and Axle Supports

1. Use glue and 4d finishing nails to attach the Sides and Ends to the Floor, butting the pieces as shown in **Figure B**.

2. Secure the Supports to the wagon box assembly using 3d finishing nails. Position one Support in each corner and two equally spaced along each side as shown in **Figure B**.

3. Assemble the Rail pieces over the wagon box and attach by driving 3d finishing nails through the Rails and into the Supports (**Figure B**). Round off the corners and all exposed edges to prevent splintering.

4. Cut a 1-inch-wide, full-length axle groove along one long edge of each Axle Support (**Figure C**). You can do this in one pass with a router, or two angled cuts with a circular saw to form a V-shaped groove.

5. On the front Axle Support only, cut a rectangular slot 5 inches long and ¾ inch deep in the center of the ungrooved long edge, as shown in **Figure D**. Drill a ¾-inch-diameter hole through the Axle Support as shown, being careful to avoid the slot and axle groove.

Two – The Steering Assembly

1. Fit the Hinge Support into the rectangular slot in the front Axle Support, attaching it with glue and 4d nails (**Figure E**). Drill a ½-inch-diameter hole through the Hinge Support as shown, and continue drilling into the Axle Support until the drill bit emerges into the ¾-inch hole.

2. Position the front Axle Support on the underside of the wagon box, aligning the holes. Insert the stove bolt through the hole in the Floor (**Figure F**), placing one metal washer under the bolt head, one between the wagon floor and the Axle Support, and one washer and the nut at the end of the bolt. Tighten the nut so that it will hold the assembly together, but allow it to swivel freely.

3. Glue the two Hinges to the Hinge Support, leaving a 1-inch space between them as shown in **Figure G**. Secure with 4d nails driven through the Hinge Support, and 8d nails through the Axle Support.

4. You have already drilled a hole near each end of the Handle. Insert the end with the larger hole between the Hinges, aligning all three holes (**Figure G**). Insert the 5-inch length of ¾-inch-diameter dowel rod (Hinge Pin) through the holes, leaving equal extensions on each side. Do not use glue, for if you do, the handle action will be permanently frozen. Do use glue to secure the remaining 7-inch length of ¾-inch-diameter dowel rod (the Handle Bar) through the hole in the other end of the Handle.

Three – Axles and Wheels

1. Position the rear Axle Support underneath the wagon floor, about 3 inches from the rear edge, centered between the sides. Attach it with glue and screws.

2. Glue the Axles to the Axle Supports, leaving equal extensions on each end. Refer to **Figure H**, and drill and counter-sink pilot screw holes through each Axle. Insert screws into the holes to secure the Axles.

3. Figure H also shows the wheel assembly. Slip one wooden Washer over the end of an Axle, pushing it all the way up to the Axle Support. Lubricate the end of the Axle and add a Wheel, followed by another wooden Washer. Secure with an Axle Pin glued into the hole near the end of the Axle. Repeat this procedure for the other three Wheels.

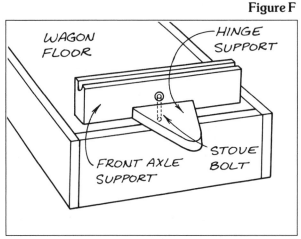

Figure F

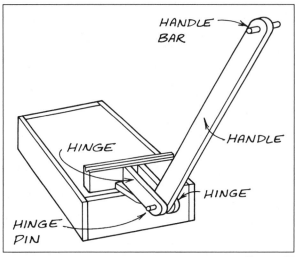

Figure G

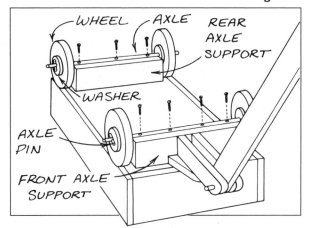

Figure H

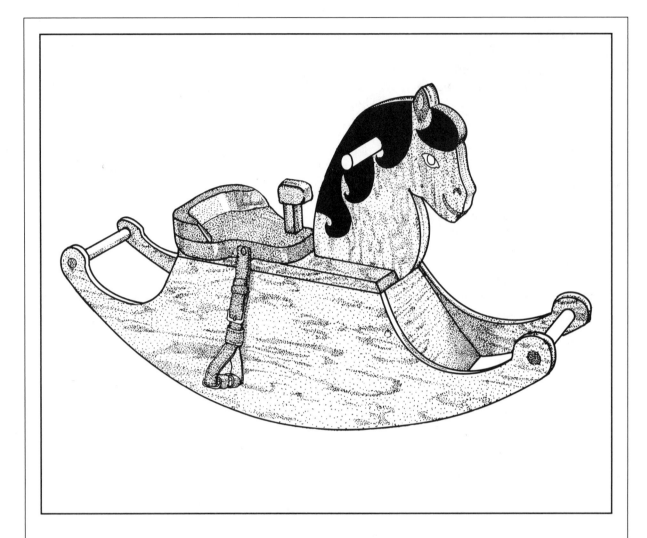

Old-Fashioned Rocking Horse

This heirloom riding toy is a western-saddle variation of an original 19th century rocking horse. A modern factory reproduction of a similar child's toy can be found in the $200 to $400 range, and an original (if you can find one) will be a bargain at anything less than $800! Enough said?

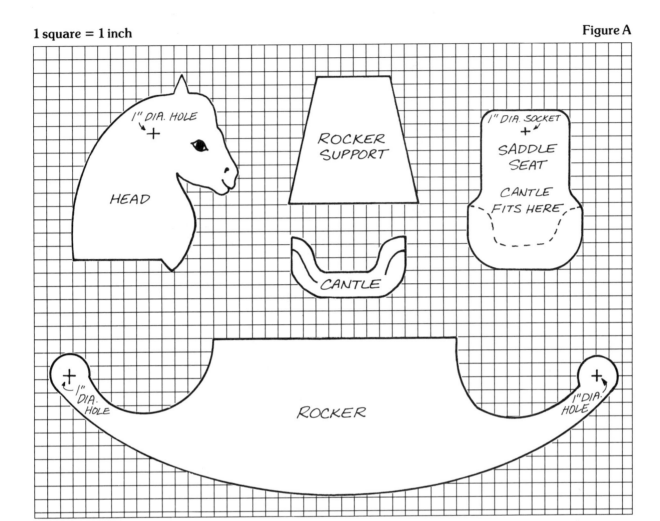

Materials

4 x 4-foot sheet of ¾-inch veneer-core plywood.

3-foot length of 1-inch-diameter wooden dowel rod.

2 linear feet of 2 x 12 pine lumber.

Handful of 1½-inch flathead wood screws; eight ⅜-inch wood screws; two 2-inch wood screws, each with a metal washer to fit; several 4d common nails; and a handful each of 3d and 4d finishing nails.

Carpenter's wood glue, wood filler, wood plugs to cover the screw holes, kraft paper and carbon paper.

Non-toxic paint in the colors of your choice and/or wood stain and varnish.

Two leather belts, each 44 inches long and 1 inch wide.

Cutting the Parts

1. Cut one Seat Platform, 19½ x 7 inches, from the ¾-inch plywood.

2. Cut the following pieces from ¾-inch plywood using the scale drawings provided in **Figure A**: two Rockers; two Rocker Supports; and two Heads. To cut two pieces exactly alike, use the enlarged paper pattern (see Tips & Techniques) to cut the first piece. Use the wooden piece as your cutting pattern for the identical twin. Round off the long curved edges of each Rocker. Cut two small Stirrup Blocks from the plywood, each 1 x 3 inches.

Figure B

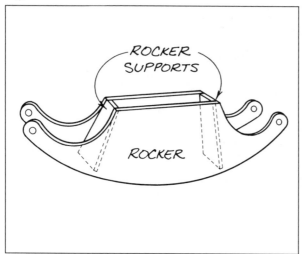

Figure C

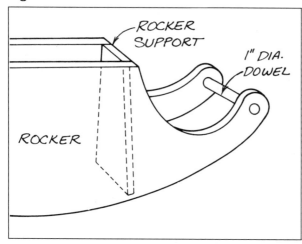

3. Cut one Saddle Seat and one Cantle (the raised back portion of the saddle assembly) from 2 x 12-inch lumber using the scale drawings in **Figure A**. Set your saw at an angle to cut the inside curved edge of the Cantle, 2 inches thick at the bottom narrowing to 1 inch thick at the top (**Figure E**). Cut one Saddle Horn Cap, 1 x 2½ inches, from a scrap piece of 2 x 12 and round all edges of this piece. Drill a 1-inch-diameter socket, 1 inch deep, into the Saddle Seat at the point marked on the scale drawing in **Figure A**, and a 1-inch-diameter socket, ½ inch deep, into one wide side of the Saddle Horn Cap.

Figure D

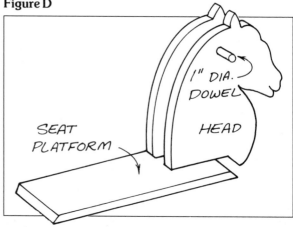

4. Cut one Handle 10 inches in length, and one Saddle Horn 4 inches in length, from the 1-inch-diameter dowel rod.

Assembly

The assembly is simple, and should be performed in three stages: first, assemble the lower section; second, the upper section; and finally, join the two sections. Use the smaller finishing nails, unless otherwise specified.

Lower Section Assembly

1. We suggest that you perform a temporary assembly on the Rockers and Rocker Supports (**Figure B**). Carefully align the Rocker Supports at the top edges of the Rockers, as shown. When the Rocker Supports are at the correct angle, they will fit flush with the bottom edge of the Rockers.

2. Drive a few temporary holding nails through the Rockers, into the edges of the Rocker Supports. If you hammer the nails completely flush with the wood, you'll be gnashing your teeth when you try to remove them later.

3. Place the assembled lower section on level ground and check the rocking action. If necessary, reposition the pieces so that the unit rocks evenly.

4. When the rocking action is smooth and even, mark the positions of the pieces, and permanently attach the Rockers to the Rocker Supports using glue and screws. Countersink the screws, and glue wood plugs over the openings.

5. Drill two dowel rod holes through each Rocker, using a 1-inch-diameter bit. Placement of the holes is indicated on the scale drawing. Bear in mind that the Rockers are assembled at an angle, so it may be necessary to enlarge the holes to accommodate the rods.

6. Connect the Rockers with sections of the 1-inch-diameter wooden dowel rod, placing one through the front of the Rockers and one through the back (**Figure C**). Both of these rods should be cut flush with the outer sides of the Rockers. Use wood filler to secure the rods in the holes.

Upper Section Assembly

1. Carefully align the two Head pieces, and glue and nail together (**Figure D**).

2. Round off both edges along the top and sides of the glued Head piece. Do not round off the bottom edges, as they will fit flush with the Seat.

3. Drill a 1-inch-diameter hole through the assembled Head at the position marked on the scale drawing. Insert the Handle and glue in place, leaving equal extensions on either side of the Head.

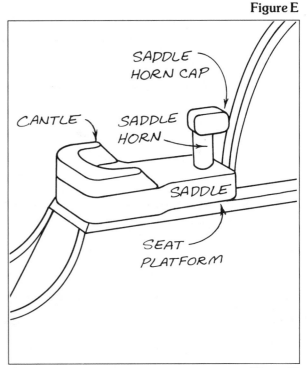

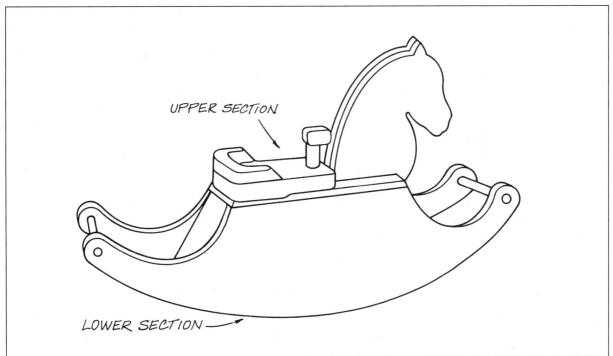

Figure G

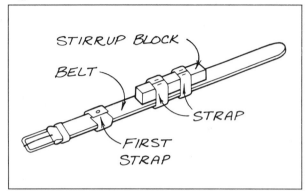

Figure H

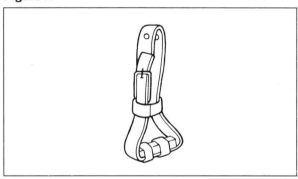

4. The assembled Head fits over the front of the Seat Platform (**Figure D**). Use the Head piece as a guide to mark and trim the front edge of the Seat Platform at an angle, so that the Head will fit flush against the edge. Use four screws to attach the Head to the Seat Platform, inserting the screws from the bottom of the Seat Platform up into the Head pieces.

5. Glue and nail the Cantle on top of the Saddle Seat, with the back edges flush (**Figure E**). Round all top edges of the saddle assembly. Glue the Saddle Horn into the socket in the Saddle Seat and the Saddle Horn Cap. Glue the assembled saddle to the Seat Platform with the back edges flush. Secure by inserting screws from the bottom of the Seat Platform up into the saddle.

Joining the Sections

1. Carefully center the upper section (Head, Seat Platform, and Saddle) over the lower section (Rocker Supports and Rockers) as shown in **Figure F**. Fasten

them together with glue and long finishing nails, or screws driven through the top of the Seat Platform. Be sure to countersink nails or screws, and fill the holes, so that young riders will escape without a scratch.

2. Sand the long edges of the Seat Platform to fit flush with the top of the Rockers.

3. Completely sand the assembled horse. Begin with medium sandpaper, and finish with fine.

Stirrups

1. Cut three Straps, each 4½ inches long, from the end of one leather belt.

2. Loosely wrap one of the Straps around the same belt and attach the ends of the Strap together with staples or a rivet. The Strap must be able to slide freely on the belt (**Figure G**).

3. Place one of the Stirrup Blocks lengthwise on the back (unfinished side) of the belt. Wrap the remaining two Straps around the belt and the Stirrup Block, attaching the loose ends of the Straps to the Stirrup Block with four ³⁄₈-inch-long screws (**Figure G**). This assembly must also be able to slide freely on the belt and should be below the first strap (step 2) or closest to the free end of the belt.

4. Measure from the end of the belt buckle and mark points at 6 and 8 inches. Drill a small hole through the belt at both of these points. Fold the belt over (finished side out) and align these two holes. Insert a 2-inch screw through a small washer, then through the hole closest to the buckle and continue through the second hole (**Figure H**).

5. Bring the free end of the belt back up (finished side out) and through the strap made in step 2, then through the buckle. Adjust the belt (excuse me, the stirrup) to your young rider before making a hole for the buckle. Slide the Stirrup Block to the bottom of the assembly and pull the free strap down to form the stirrup.

6. Repeat these procedures to make a second stirrup.

7. Stain and varnish, or paint with a non-toxic paint. Allow the assembly to dry before attaching the stirrups to the sides of the saddle, using the 2-inch screws.

8. Paint the mane and facial features.

Install a budding cowpolk on the finished horse, and let'er rip!

Pumpmobile

If we could figure out how to harness the excess energy that every child under the age of ten seems to possess, we could say goodbye to oil, natural gas, hydro-electric, and nuclear power altogether. It has always seemed a little wasteful to put a 20-horsepower child on a ½-horsepower go-cart or mini-bike. The Pumpmobile puts a little of that natural locomotion power where it belongs – having fun.

Figure A

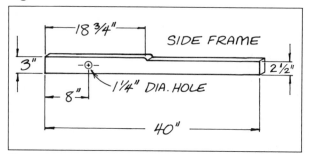

Figure B

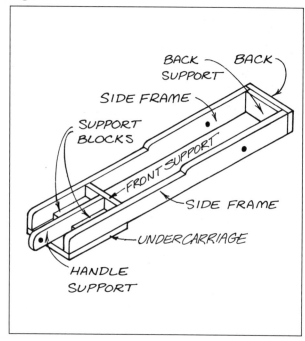

Materials

2 x 2-foot piece of ½-inch exterior plywood.
Two 22 x 28-inch pieces of 1-inch exterior plywood.
18 linear feet of 1 x 4 pine.
1 linear foot of 2 x 4 pine.
2 linear feet of 2 x 2 pine.
2-foot length of ⅜-inch dowel rod.
1-foot length of ¾-inch dowel rod.
5-foot length of 1-inch dowel rod.
4d finishing nails.
Used plastic bottles to be cut into washers.

Cutting the Parts

1. Cut the following pieces from ½-inch plywood:

Description	Dimensions	Quantity
Seat	10 x 12 inches	1
Seat Support	8 x 11 inches	2
Seat Side	2½ x 10½ inches	2
Seat Back	2½ x 12 inches	1

2. Cut the following pieces from 1-inch plywood:

Description	Dimensions	Quantity
Spacer Block	2¾ x 3 inches	2
Undercarriage	7⅞ x 10½ inches	1
Front Wheel	7-inch diameter	4
Rear Wheel	13-inch diameter	4

3. Glue and clamp together the Front Wheels in sets of two, so you have two 2-inch-thick Front Wheels. Do the same with the Rear Wheels.

4. Cut the following pieces from the 1-inch dowel:

Description	Length	Quantity
Drive Axle	6 inches	1
Front Axle	5 inches	2
Rear Axle	4½ inches	2
Handle Bar	11½ inches	1
Steering Pivot	5½ inches	1

5. Cut seven Axle Pins, each 3 inches long, from ⅜-inch wooden dowel.

6. Cut two Handle Connectors, each 2½ inches long, from ¾-inch wooden dowel.

7. Cut the following pieces from 1 x 4 lumber:

Description	Dimensions	Quantity
Handle	2¾ x 21 inches	2
Drive Shaft	3 x 36½ inches	1
Stabilizers	2¾-inch diameter	5
Handle Support	2½ x 13 inches	1
Side Frame	3 x 40 inches	2
Back	3 x 7⅞ inches	1
Support Block	2¾ x 6 inches	2
Back Support	3 x 6⅜ inches	1
Front Support	2½ x 6⅜ inches	1

Figure C

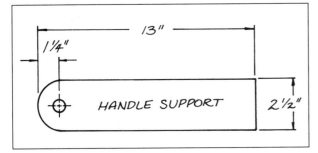

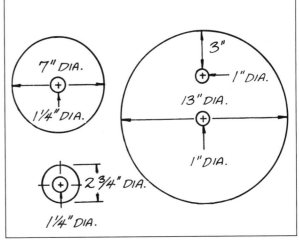

8. Cut one Steering Bar, 24 inches long, from 2 x 2.

9. Cut one Braking Block, 9 inches long, from 2 x 4.

10. Cut seven Washers, each 3 inches in diameter, from plastic (old bleach bottles, etc.). During the assembly process, you can cut a center hole in each to match the dowel on which it is to fit.

Assembly

1. Contour each Side Frame piece as shown in **Figure A**. Temporarily nail the two Side Frame pieces together and drill a 1¼-inch hole through both pieces, centered 8 inches from the back. Remove the nails holding the two pieces together.

2. The frame assembly is shown in **Figure B**. Nail the Back piece across the back ends of the Side Frames. Glue and nail the Back Support between the Side Frames and against the Back.

3. Attach the Undercarriage to the bottoms of the Frame Sides, flush with the front ends. Mount the Front Support between the Frame Sides and flush with the back edge of the Undercarriage. Nail and glue the Support Blocks in position as shown in **Figure B**. The Braking Block is nailed across the bottom of the Undercarriage, approximately 1 inch from the back edge to keep the Front Wheels from rubbing against the Side Frames when steering.

4. Round one end of the Handle Support (**Figure C**). Measure back 1¼ inches from the rounded end and drill a 1¼-inch-diameter hole. Glue and nail the Handle Support between the Support Blocks and butted against the Front Support.

5. Refer to **Figure D** as you drill the Wheels and all Wheel Stabilizers. Temporarily nail together the two Front Wheels and drill the 1¼-inch-diameter axle holes

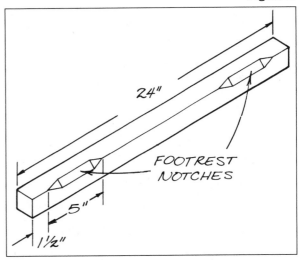

simultaneously. Each Back Wheel has a 1-inch-diameter center axle hole and a 1-inch-diameter hole drilled for the Drive Axle. Drill the Drive Axle hole 3 inches from the outside edge as shown. The Front Wheels have a 1¼-inch-diameter axle hole to insure that they will rotate freely around the 1-inch Front Axles.

6. The 2-foot length of 2 x 2 will serve as the Steering Bar. Cut a 5-inch-wide footrest notch into the Steering Bar, 1½ inches from each end (**Figure E**). These cutouts will be at the top rear edges of the Steering Bar, facing the driver.

Figure F

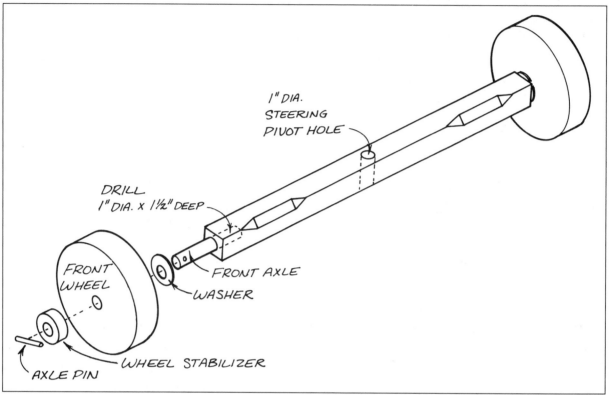

1" DIA.
STEERING
PIVOT HOLE

DRILL
1" DIA. X 1½" DEEP

FRONT AXLE

FRONT
WHEEL

WASHER

WHEEL STABILIZER

AXLE PIN

Figure G

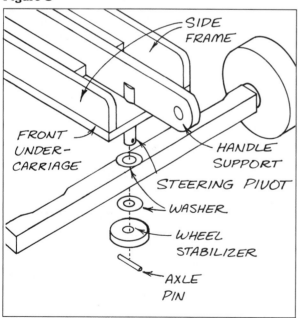

SIDE
FRAME

FRONT
UNDER-
CARRIAGE

HANDLE
SUPPORT

STEERING PIVOT

WASHER

WHEEL
STABILIZER

AXLE
PIN

7. Figure F shows the front axle assembly. Drill a 1-inch-diameter socket, 1½ inches deep into each end of the Steering Bar for the Front Axles. Drill an additional 1-inch-diameter hole down through the Steering Bar for the Steering Pivot as shown. Glue the Front Axles into the sockets. Mount a Washer, a Front Wheel, and a Stabilizer on each Front Axle. Drill a ⅜-inch hole through each Front Axle and insert and glue an Axle Pin to secure the assembly.

8. Measure 1½ inches from the front edge of the Undercarriage and drill a 1-inch-diameter socket, 2 inches deep, up through the Undercarriage and into the Handle Support (**Figure G**). Glue the Steering Pivot into this hole. Mount a Washer over the Steering Pivot, then insert the Pivot through the hole drilled in the Steering Bar. Install another Washer, a Stabilizer, and another Washer. Drill a ⅜-inch-diameter hole through the Steering Pivot below this assembly and glue an Axle Pin in place.

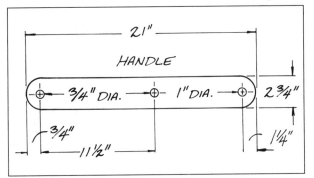

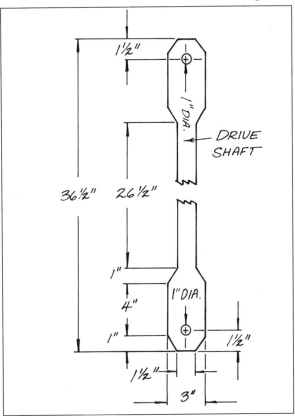

9. Temporarily nail the two Handle pieces together and round both ends (**Figure H**). Measure from one end and mark points at ¾ inch and 12¼ inches. Drill ¾-inch-diameter holes through both Handles at these points. Measure 1¼ inches from the opposite end and drill a 1-inch-diameter hole through both Handle pieces. Now separate the two pieces by removing the temporary nails.

10. A cutting diagram for the Drive Shaft is provided in **Figure I**. Modify the Drive Shaft piece as shown and then measure in 1½ inches from each end of the Drive Shaft and drill 1-inch-diameter holes (**Figure H**).

11. Refer to **Figure J** as you assemble the Rear Wheels. Insert the Drive Axle through one end of the Drive Shaft, leaving equal extensions on each side. Mount a Rear Wheel on either end of the Drive Axle, the Drive Axle going into the offset holes (not the center holes) and coming flush with the outside of the wheels. Drill ⅜-inch-diameter holes through the Drive Axle, flush with the inside of the wheels, and glue and insert Axle Pins.

12. Refer to **Figure K** as you install the rear wheel assembly on the frame. Place the rear wheel assembly between the Frame Sides with the Drive Shaft over the frame assembly. Insert one Rear Axle through the hole drilled in the Frame Side. Mount a Washer on the axle inside the frame, and glue the axle into one of the Rear Wheels (center hole) so that the axle is flush with the inside of the wheel. Mount a Stabilizer over the outer end of the axle, and drill a ⅜-inch-diameter hole for an Axle Pin as shown in **Figure K**. Glue the Axle Pin into position. Repeat this for the other Rear Axle/Rear Wheel assembly.

Figure J

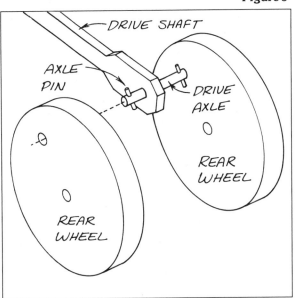

Figure K

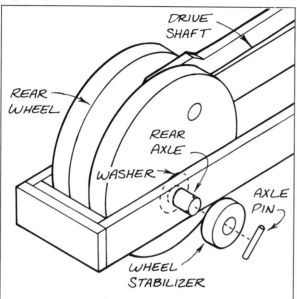

Figure M

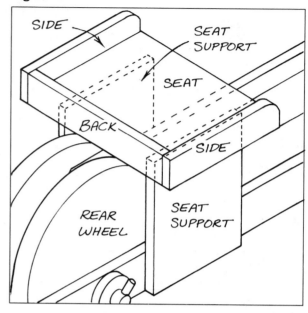

Figure L

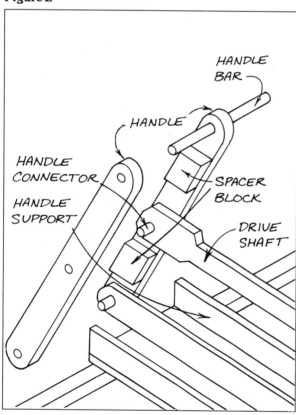

13. Refer to **Figure L** as you install the Handles on the free end of the Drive Shaft. Glue the Spacer Blocks to one of the Handle pieces as shown. Insert a Handle Connector dowel into the ¾-inch-diameter hole at one end of this Handle, and through the Handle Support piece attached to the frame assembly. Hold the Drive Shaft in position and insert another Handle Connector through the middle hole in the Handle, and through the Drive Shaft. Insert and glue the Handle Bar into the 1-inch-diameter hole in the Handle. Install the remaining Handle over the ends of the dowels as shown in **Figure L**. The lower Handle Connector dowel should be glued to the Handles only, not to the Handle Support. The upper Connector dowel should also be glued to the Handles only, not to the Drive Shaft. Firmly secure the Handle pieces together by nailing through both Handle pieces into the Spacer Blocks.

14. Position the Seat Supports on the outside of the Side Frames and 12 inches from the Back, flush with the bottom of the frame. Assemble the seat pieces as shown in **Figure M**. Adjust the seat on top of the supports to accommodate your child.

15. The Pumpmobile should now look like the finished assembly in **Figure N**.

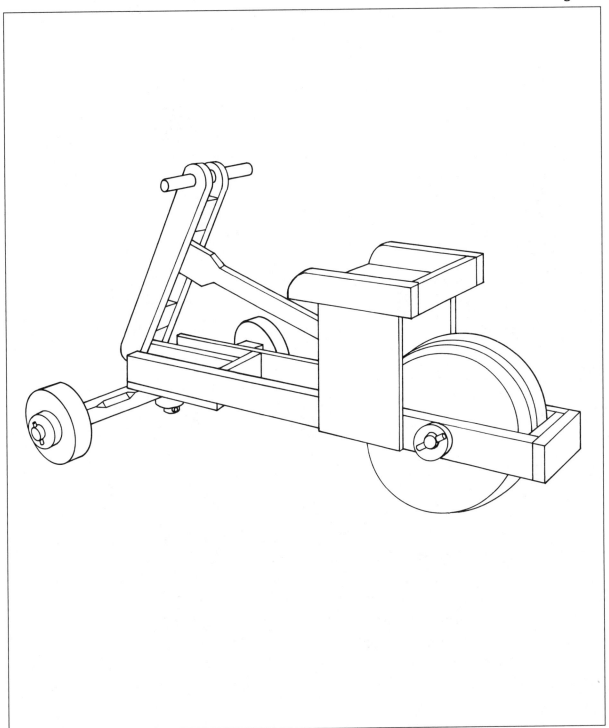

Horsey Trike

Have you ever heard of "planned obsolescence?" We believe the folks who manufacture children's plastic riding toys must have invented the phrase. One (good?) year and they take up permanent residence at the city dump. Our Horsey Trike is a push toy that will end up as something that Great-Grandad played with. A fresh coat of paint every generation or so and this riding toy will keep right on rolling along.

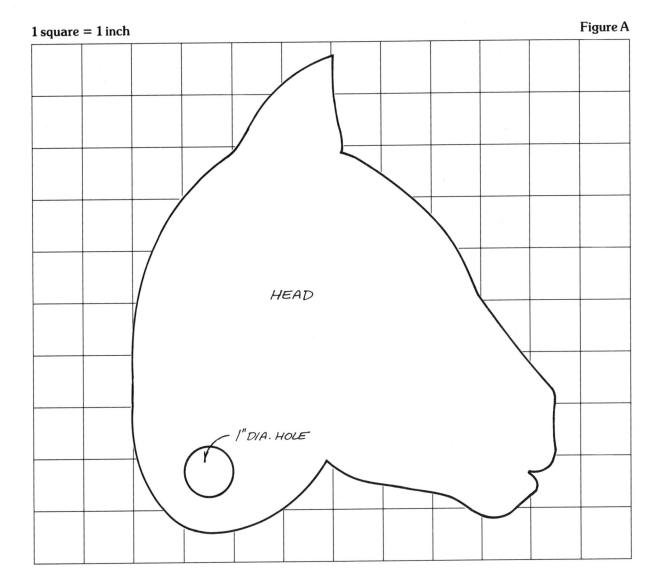

Materials

2 linear feet of 1 x 10 lumber.
2 linear feet of 1 x 8 lumber.
1 linear foot of 1 x 6 lumber.
6 linear feet of 1 x 4 lumber.
3 linear feet of 2 x 4 lumber.
1 linear foot of 2 x 2 lumber.
3-foot length of ½-inch wooden dowel.
2-foot length of 1-inch wooden dowel.
2 x 2-foot piece of ½-inch plywood for the wheels.

(We laminated the plywood into 1½-inch thickness before cutting three 7-inch-diameter wheels. If you wish, the wheels can be cut from a 2-foot length of 2 x 8 lumber, or you may substitute old lawnmower wheels.)
Eight metal washers having ⅝-inch center holes.
Sixteen plastic washers – these can be cut from old bleach or detergent bottles.
3-foot length of ½-inch-diameter sisal rope.
4d and 8d finishing nails.
Carpenter's glue.

Figure B

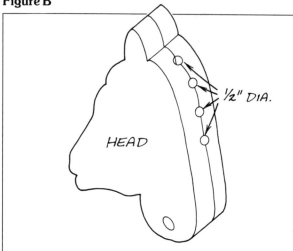

½" DIA.

HEAD

Cutting the Parts

1. The horse's head is cut from 1 x 10 lumber using the scale drawing in **Figure A**. Cut two Heads and glue them together with all edges flush. Drill a 1-inch-diameter hole for the Handle Bar through both pieces at the point specified. Drill four evenly spaced ½-inch-diameter sockets, ½ inch deep, along the back edge (the mane) of the assembled head (**Figure B**).

2. The Seat is cut from 1 x 8 lumber using the scale drawing in **Figure C**. Label the Seat: part **A**.

3. The Seat Back is cut from 1 x 6 lumber using the scale drawing in **Figure C**. Label the Seat Back: B.

4. Cut and label the following pieces from 1 x 4 lumber using the scale drawings in **Figure C**. Drill holes at points and in sizes specified.

Figure C

1 square = 1 inch

SWIVEL
F

SEAT
SUPPORT
G

SHOULDER
D

FRONT RAIL
C

BACK RAIL
E

SEAT
BACK
B

SEAT
A

Description	Code	Length	Quantity
Front Rails	C	15¼ inches	2
Shoulders	D	2½ inches	2
Back Rails	E	9 inches	2
Swivels	F	6 inches	2
Seat Supports	G	3½ inches	2

5. Cut and label the following pieces from 2 x 2 lumber for the rear axle spacer blocks, then drill a ½-inch-diameter hole lengthwise through each piece (**Figure D**).

Description	Code	Length	Quantity
Center Block	H	3 inches	1
Outer Blocks	I	2¼ inches	2

6. Cut and label the following pieces from 2 x 4 lumber. After cutting the Strut to length, mark a point on one 1½-inch edge, ¾ inch from one end. Drill a ½-inch-diameter hole through the Strut at this point (refer to **Figure E**).

Description	Code	Length	Quantity
Strut	J	18 inches	1
Swivel Blocks	K	3¾ inches	2
Head Block	L	3 inches	1

7. Cut and label the following pieces from ½-inch-diameter wooden dowel:

Description	Code	Length	Quantity
Front Axle	M	6 inches	1
Rear Axle	N	13 inches	1
Swivel Bar	O	5¼ inches	1

8. Cut and label the following pieces from 1-inch-diameter wooden dowel. Drill a ½-inch-diameter socket, ¾ inch deep into one end of each Hub Cap. Drill a ⅝-inch-diameter hole completely through the center of each Axle Spacer (**Figure F**).

Description	Code	Length	Quantity
Handle Bar	P	10 inches	1
Hub Caps	Q	1¼ inches	4
Axle Spacers	R	⅝ inch	2

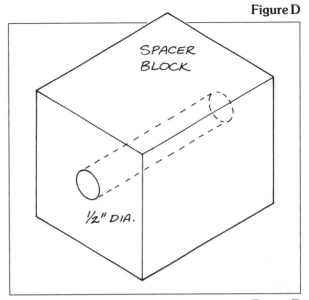

Figure D

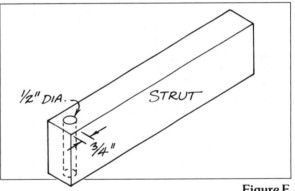

Figure E

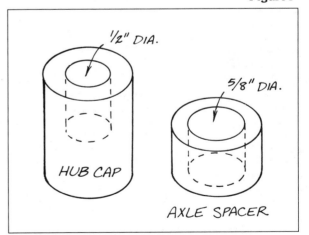

Figure F

Figure G

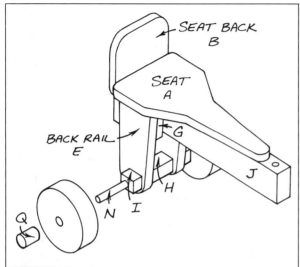

SEAT BACK
B

SEAT
A

BACK RAIL
E

G

J

H

N   I

Q

Figure H

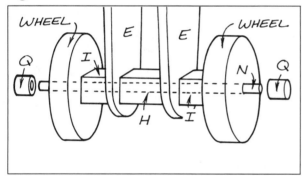

WHEEL

E   E

WHEEL

Q   I

N   Q

H   I

Figure I

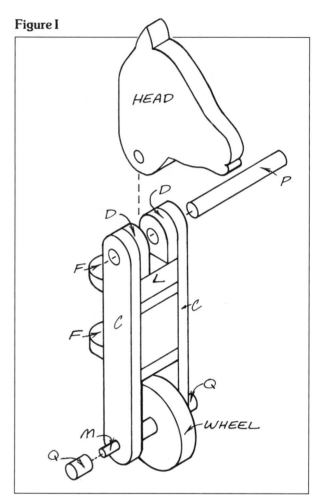

HEAD

P

D

D

F

L

C

F   C

C

Q

WHEEL

M

Q

---

9. Cut the following lengths of rope for the horse's mane and tail:

Mane – four pieces, each 6 inches long
Tail – one piece, 12 inches long

Assembly

1. Assemble the rear portion as shown in **Figure G**. A detail of the rear wheel assembly is shown in **Figure H**. To begin, glue the H, E and I pieces to the N axle with equal portions of the axle extending from each side, as shown.

2. Mount a plastic washer, a metal washer, and another plastic washer on both sides of each wheel to insure the least amount of wear. Secure the wheel assembly by glueing Q Hub Caps to the ends of the axle.

The wheels should rotate freely around the axle.

3. A G piece is glued to the inside of each E piece, with the tops and backs flush.

4. Position the rear of the J piece (the end without a hole drilled through) between the two G pieces with the top and back edges flush. Secure by driving 8d nails through the E and G pieces and into the J piece.

5. Nail the Seat (A) and Seat Back (B) to this assembly as shown.

6. The Strut (piece J) connects the front and rear assemblies. The hole drilled in one end of the J piece is positioned vertically at the front of the trike. The Swivel Bar (dowel piece O) is NOT glued to the Strut, so that the Strut may turn freely around it.

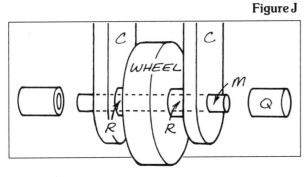

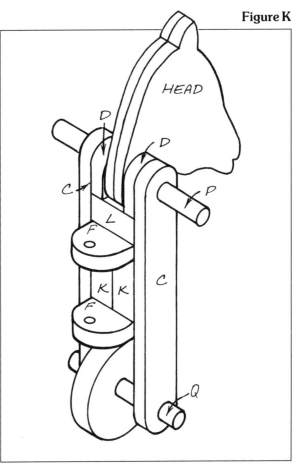

7. Refer to **Figure I** as you assemble the front portion of the trike. A detail of the front axle assembly is shown in **Figure J**. Insert the **M** dowel piece through the ½-inch-diameter hole in one **C** piece, through a **R** piece, a wheel, then another **R** piece and through the matching **C** piece. Secure the axle assembly by glueing Hub Caps (**Q**) to both ends of the axle.

8. Glue one **D** piece to the inside of each **C** piece with the top rounded edges flush. Position the horse's head between the two **D** pieces and insert the **P** Handle Bar through the assembly. Note: DO NOT glue the head in place, it should be free to rock back and forth on the Handle Bar.

9. Nail the two **K** pieces vertically between the unrounded ends of the two **F** pieces (**Figure K**). Nail the **L** piece horizontally to the top of one **F** piece, flush with the unrounded end. Position this assembly between the **C** pieces with the **L** piece butting against the bottoms of the **D** pieces. Secure the two assemblies by nailing through the sides of the **C** pieces into the **F**, **K**, and **L** pieces.

10. Insert the **O** dowel piece into the hole in the top **F** piece. Add a plastic washer, a metal washer, and another plastic washer before you run the dowel through the **J** Strut, then another set of washers before glueing the dowel into the bottom **F** piece (**Figure L**).

11. Sand all exposed corners and sharp edges to prevent large tears from small people.

12. Paint or finish as desired. Make sure you don't get paint where it will freeze up any moving parts.

13. Glue and nail strands of rope into the holes drilled in the back of the head for the mane, and a longer length at the back for the tail.

14. Stand back 'cause the little guys will run right over you!

Figure L

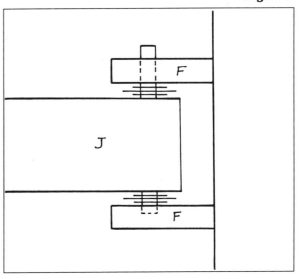

Towncar

We created the Towncar for those little folk who like to take their dates for a cruise down the sidewalk boulevard, or are into car-pooling with a friend. There is plenty of trunk space for essentials (peanut butter sandwiches and/or twenty frogs) and even an opening "engine" compartment for young mechanics to work on the 1-K.P. (Kid-Power) pedal mechanism and working steering.

Materials

25 square feet of ¾-inch pine. We used standard 1 x 12 lumber.

15 square feet of ⅛-inch plywood, with both sides finished smooth.

9 square inches of 2-inch pine. A 3 x 3-inch scrap piece will do.

8¾ x 10½-inch sheet of copper plate.

Wooden dowel rod: 14 feet of ¼-inch, and a 24-inch length of 1-inch.

Six eyescrews, each approximately ½ inch in diameter and 3 inches long.

Three piano hinges: one 7 inches long, and two 12 inches long, each with screws to fit.

Two metal conduit clamps that will accommodate ½-inch-diameter pipe.

Metal axle rods: one straight rod for the front axle, ½ inch in diameter and 20 inches long; and one rod for the rear drive axle, ½ inch in diameter and 30 inches long, threaded on the ends and bent as shown in **Figure A**. If you're not confident about bending this rod yourself, ask for help at a hardware shop, metal shop, or service station. The straight axle rod will need to be drilled through, ¼ inch from each end, to accommodate the cotter pins that hold the wheels in place. If you do not have a drill that will do the job, one of the shops listed above will be able to perform the task for you. The bent drive axle will also need to be drilled through to accommodate cotter pins, 2 inches from each end.

Two locknuts to fit the ends of the drive axle.

Four cotter pins.

Eight flat metal washers, each with a ⅝-inch-diameter center hole.

Nine machine bolts: one 4½ inches long, ⅜ inch in diameter, with two flat washers, one spring lock washer, and a nut to fit; four bolts, each 2 inches long and ¼ inch in diameter, each with three flat washers and a nut to fit; and four bolts, each 2½ inches long and ¼ inch in diameter, each with two flat washers and a nut to fit.

Two sheet metal screws, each ¾ inch long, with flat washers.

Decorative upholstery tacks.

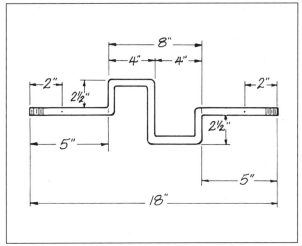

Figure A

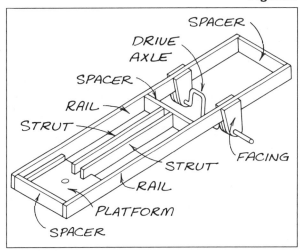

Figure B

6-foot length of ⅛-inch-diameter plastic covered cable.

Finishing nails, No. 6 gauge flathead wood screws, carpenter's wood glue, wood filler, beeswax or other lubricant, non-toxic paint in your choice of colors, and pattern paper (wrapping paper, grocery sacks, or drafting paper with a grid of 1-inch squares).

1 yard of black vinyl or heavy cloth.

One bag of polyester fiberfill.

Building the Frame

The assembled frame is shown in **Figure B**. Refer to this diagram as you work through this section.

Figure C 1 square = 1 inch

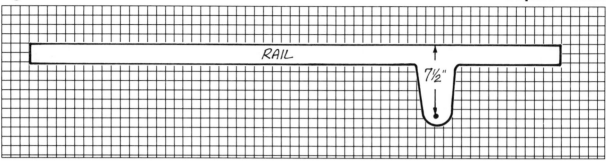

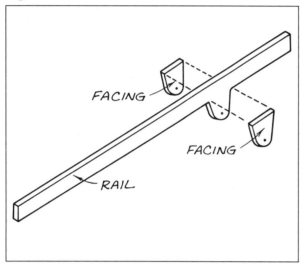

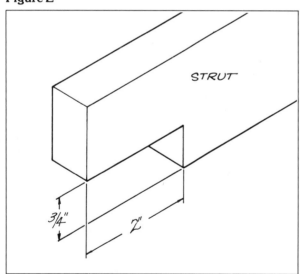

1. A scale drawing of the Rail is provided in **Figure C**. Enlarge the drawing to make a full-size paper pattern, and cut two Frames from ¾-inch pine. It's important that the two Rails be identical, so the axle holes will line up properly. To accomplish this we suggest you begin by cutting two 9 x 59-inch rectangles from ¾-inch pine, nail them together temporarily, and cut the pieces simultaneously. In addition, drill a ½-inch-diameter axle hole through both pieces, centered on the axle extension, 7½ inches from the upper edge. Remove the temporary holding nails and separate the Rails.

2. Each Rail is reinforced by plywood Facings, which are cut to match the rear portion (**Figure D**). Cut four 6 x 9-inch plywood pieces, and nail them together temporarily. Use the rear portion of one wooden Rail as a pattern to cut the Facings and to drill the axle holes.

3. Glue and nail a plywood Facing to each side of one Rail (**Figure D**). Attach the remaining Facings to the other Rail.

4. Three Spacers serve to connect the two Rails. Cut three Spacers from ¾-inch pine, each 2 x 10½ inches.

5. Align the two Rails and insert one end of the bent drive axle into the rear hole in each one. Glue one Spacer between the Rails flush with the back ends as shown in **Figure B**. Glue one of the remaining Spacers between the Rails flush with the front ends. Insert and glue the remaining Spacer between the Rails 35¼ inches from the front end. Secure the Spacers in place using screws.

6. A Platform is attached between the Rails at the front of the frame. It serves to hold the front end of the steering assembly, and the axle assembly is suspended from it. Cut one Platform 7½ x 10½ inches from

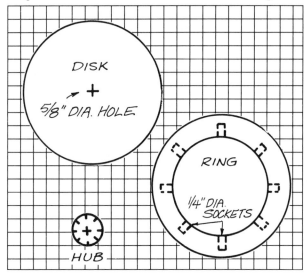

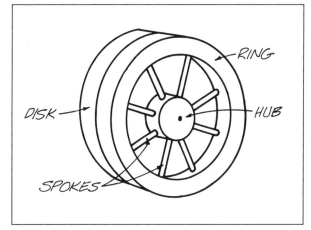

¾-inch pine. In addition, cut two Braces from the same material, each 1¼ x 7½ inches. Drill a ½-inch-diameter hole through the Platform 1¼ inches from one long edge and centered between the sides. This hole will accommodate the bolt that supports the axle assembly.

7. Glue the Platform between the two Rails flush against the front Spacer, placing the bolt hole toward the rear (**Figure B**). The bottom of the Platform should be flush with the bottom edges of the Rails. Glue the Braces on top of the Platform, flush against the front Spacer and the Rails. Secure these joints with screws.

8. Two Struts are attached to the frame to support the pedal assemblies. Cut two Struts from ¾-inch pine, each 2 x 29 inches. Cut a ¾ x 2-inch notch in one end of each Strut, as shown in **Figure E**. Place the Struts between the middle Spacer and the back edge of the Platform (**Figure B**), centered between the two Rails and allowing a 1½-inch space between them. Temporarily secure both ends with screws.

Wheel Assembly

Each assembled wheel consists of one Disk, one Hub, one Ring, and eight Spokes. An assembled wheel is shown in **Figure G**.

1. Cut the following pieces from ¾-inch pine: four circular Disks, each 11 inches in diameter; four circular

Hubs, each 2¼ inches in diameter; and four Rings, using the scale drawing provided in **Figure F**. Cut thirty-two Spokes, each 3½ inches long, from the ¼-inch dowel.

2. Drill eight evenly-spaced ¼-inch-diameter holes completely through one of the 11-inch Rings, from the outer edge to the inner edge. Drill eight evenly spaced ¼-inch-diameter sockets, ¼-inch-deep, into the edge of one of the 2¼-inch Hubs. Insert eight Spokes through the holes in the Ring and connect with the sockets in the Hub. Glue the Spokes in place and fill the holes in the Ring with wood filler. Glue and clamp this assembly over one of the 11-inch Disks.

3. Repeat the procedures in step 2 to make three additional wheels.

4. Measure carefully to the exact center of each assembled wheel. Drill a ⅝-inch-diameter hole through both the Hub and the Disk of two of the wheels for the front axle, and drill a ½-inch-diameter hole through each remaining wheel for the rear drive axle.

Rear Axles and Pedal Assembly

A diagram of the finished pedal mechanism is provided in **Figure J**.

1. The bent drive axle is already in place. When the pedals are pushed, this axle rotates to turn the rear wheels. For this reason, the wheels on the drive axle must be secured tightly so they will spin as the axle does. Perform the following procedures at each end

Figure H

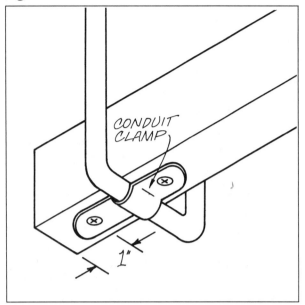

CONDUIT CLAMP

1"

Figure I

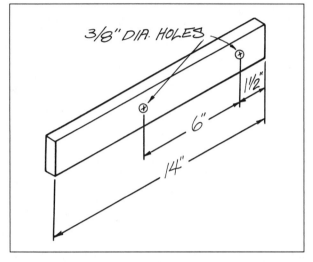

3/8" DIA. HOLES

1½"

6"

14"

of the drive axle. First, insert a cotter pin through the hole that was drilled 2 inches from the end. Add a washer, a wheel, and another washer. Install a locknut and tighten until the wheels are securely wedged against the inner washer and cotter pin.

2. Cut the following pieces from ¾-inch pine for the pedal mechanism: two Connecting Bars, each 2 x 28 inches; two Pedal Bars, each 2 x 14 inches; and two Pedals, each 3 x 4 inches. Round off all four corners of each pedal.

3. The Connecting Bars are attached to the drive axle at one end, and to the Pedal Bars at the opposite end. To attach one Connecting Bar to the drive axle, attach one flange of a metal conduit clamp 1 inch from one end of the lower edge of the Bar, as shown in **Figure H**. Place the Connecting Bar over one throw of the axle and slip the clamp over the axle as shown. Install the remaining clamp flange on the Connecting Bar. Attach the other Connecting Bar to the opposite drive axle throw in the same manner.

4. A hole drilled through the Connecting Bar near the opposite end will accommodate the pivot bolt that joins the Connecting Bar to the Pedal Bar. Drill a ⅜-inch-diameter hole through the Connecting Bar, 1½ inches from the front end.

5. Drill two ⅜-inch-diameter holes through each Pedal Bar: one 1½ inches from one short end, and one 6 inches from the first hole, measuring center to center, as shown in **Figure I**.

6. Join one of the Pedal Bars to the outer side of each Connecting Bar in the following manner: First, slip a washer over the end of a 2-inch-long bolt. Insert the bolt through the hole near the front of the Connecting Bar, add another washer, and install the nut. Be sure to leave this assembly loose enough to rotate.

7. Rotate the drive axle until the back end of one Connecting Bar is at the very bottom of its rotation cycle. The other Connecting Bar will now be at the very top of its cycle. Chock the wheels so the axle will not turn as you work. At the front end of the Connecting Bar that is at the bottom of its cycle, move the Pedal Bar to a vertical position. Place the Pedal Bar against the outer side of the frame Center Strut (**Figure J**) and adjust it up or down until the open hole in the Pedal Bar is midway between the top and the bottom edges of the Strut. (Make sure the Bar is still in a vertical position.) Mark the position of the hole on the Strut and drill a ⅜-inch-diameter hole through the Strut at this point. Slip a washer over the end of a 2-inch-long bolt and insert the bolt through the Pedal Bar. Add another washer, insert the bolt through the Strut, add a third washer, and install the nut, leaving the assembly loose enough to pivot.

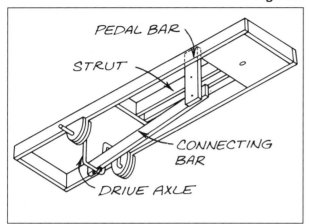

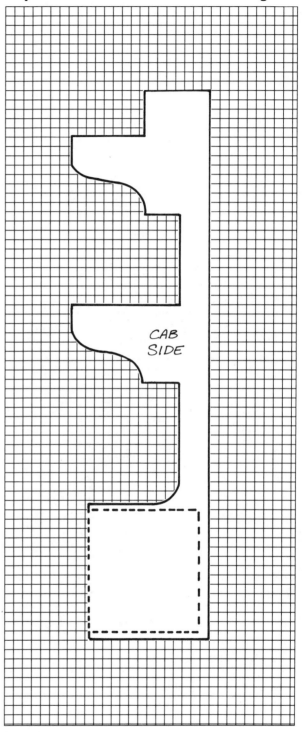

CAB
SIDE

8. Rotate the drive axle one-half turn, so that the free Connecting Bar is at the bottom of its cycle, and repeat the procedures in step 7 to join the remaining Connecting Bar to the remaining Pedal Bar and Strut.

Note: It may be necessary to trim the tops of the Pedal Bars to make them a more comfortable length for your child. The Pedals, therefore, will be attached after you have built the cab, and can "fit" the Pedal Bars to the pint-size driver.

Building the Cab

The cab consists of plywood sides and hood assembly, and ¾-inch pine seats and trunk assemblies as shown in **Figure L**.

1. We suggest you cut the Cab Sides simultaneously, as you did the Frame pieces. A scale drawing of the Cab Side is provided in **Figure K**. Enlarge the drawing to make a full-size paper pattern and cut two Cab Sides from plywood. The area indicated by a dotted line will be the Engine Compartment Door and should be cut and separated from the Cab Sides. In addition, cut one Hood from the same material, 13½ x 14 inches.

2. Cut two Seat Backs from ¾-inch pine, each 13 x 12 inches. Since this is probably wider than your stock, it will be necessary to spline (or simply glue and clamp) two pieces together to create each Seat Back.

3. Begin the cab assembly by glueing the Cab Sides to the outer sides of the Frame pieces, with the front and lower edges flush. Secure the Sides with screws.

Figure L

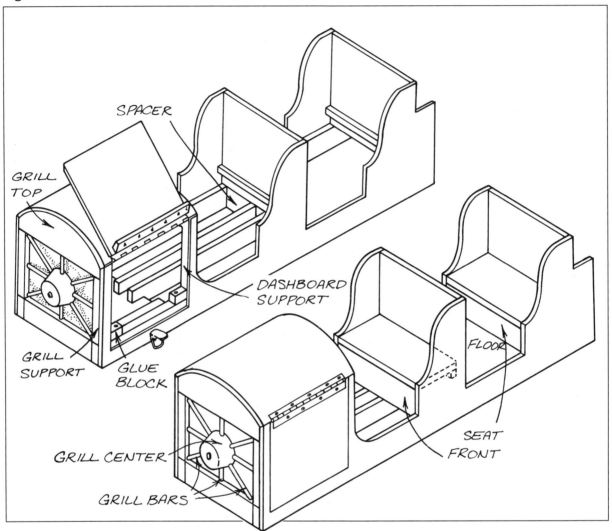

4. Insert and glue the Seat Backs between the Cab Sides so that they rest on top of the Frame pieces, flush with the back of each seat portion of the Cab Sides. The front Seat Back will rest directly on top of the middle Spacer. Secure with finishing nails driven through the Cab Sides.

5. Cut the following pieces from ¾-inch pine: two Seats, each 7½ x 11⅞ inches; one Seat Front (for the rear seat) 4¼x 12 inches; one Seat Front (for the front seat) 5 x 12 inches; and one Floor, 10 x 12 inches.

6. Refer to **Figure L** as you complete the seat as-

semblies. The Floor is for the passenger. It rests between the Cab Sides, on top of the Frame pieces, behind the front seat. Glue and nail each Seat Front between the Cab Sides, flush with the vertical edges of the Sides at the front of each "seat" portion. The passengers Seat Front is 4¼ inches tall and rests on top of the Floor. The driver's Seat Front is 5 inches tall and rests directly on the Frame. Round off the corners of the Seat pieces and place each one between the Cab Sides so that it rests on top of the Seat Front and butts against the Seat Back. Secure with glue and nails.

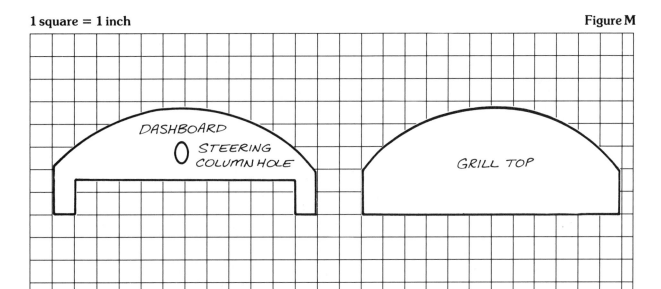

7. The front portion of the cab consists of the Hood, the Dashboard, the front grill assembly and the engine compartment Doors. Scale drawings for the Dashboard and Grill Top are provided in **Figure M**. Enlarge the drawings to make full-sized paper patterns and cut one of each piece from ¾-inch pine. The hole that is shown in the Dashboard will accommodate the Steering Column, and should be drilled at a downward angle as shown in **Figure N**.

8. To assemble the grill and dashboard sections, cut the following pieces from ¾-inch pine: two Dashboard Supports and two Grill Supports, each ¾ x 8¾ inches, and four rectangular glue blocks, each 1½ x 1 inch. Glue the four Supports, with blocks behind, atop the Frame (**Figure L**), between the Cab Sides and flush with the outside edges of the "engine compartment." On top of these supports, mount the Grill Top and Dashboard. Drive small nails through the Cab Sides, into the Supports, the Grill Top, and the Dashboard. The Grill Top, Grill Supports, and frame Spacer now form a frame for the grill.

9. Along the inside back edges of the grill frame, attach small strips of wood against which the 8¾ x 10½-inch copper Grill Backing will rest.

10. Drill eight ¼-inch-diameter sockets, ¼-inch-deep, into the grill frame for the dowel rod grill bars.

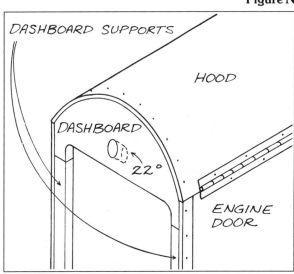

Drill one socket diagonally into each corner, one into each Support, one into the frame Spacer, and one into the Grill Top, each half-way between the corners (**Figure L**). Cut a 3-inch circle from a 2-inch-thick piece of wood. This will be the Grill Center. Around the outside edge, at even intervals, drill eight ¼-inch-diameter sockets, ½ inch deep. Cut eight lengths of ¼-inch wooden dowel: two 3½ inchs long; two 4¼ inches long; and four 5¾ inches long.

Figure O

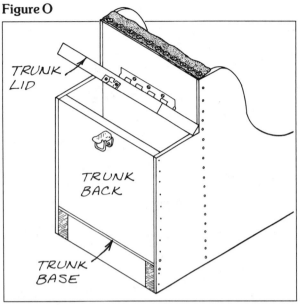

TRUNK LID

TRUNK BACK

TRUNK BASE

Figure P　　　　　　　　　　1 square = 1 inch

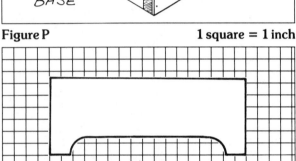

11. Insert the dowel rod Grill Bars into the Grill Center: the two 3½-inch pieces at what will be the top and bottom; the 4¼-inch pieces on the left and right sides; and the four 5¾-inch pieces at the corners. Place the Grill Backing into the grill frame. Position the grill bar assembly in front of the Grill Backing and slide the bars outward until they fit into the sockets in the grill frame. Glue them in place.

12. The Hood is a 13½ x 14-inch piece of ⅛-inch plywood. Place one 14-inch edge over the Grill Top and the Dashboard at the point where they start to curve. Nail this edge down and bend the Hood along the Grill Top and Dashboard, nailing it down as you go.

13. The engine compartment Doors are attached to the Hood using the two 12-inch piano hinges.

Figure Q

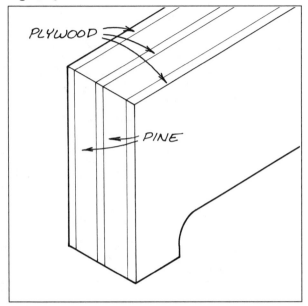

PLYWOOD

PINE

14. Cut the following pieces from ¾-inch pine to construct the trunk of the towncar: one 8 x 12-inch Trunk Back, and one 12¼ x 5-inch Trunk Lid. Cut one 4¼ x 12-inch Trunk Base from ⅛-inch plywood.

15. Refer to **Figure O** as you assemble the trunk. Mount the Trunk Base on top of the Frame Sides, flush with the back edge of the frame Spacer. Attach the Trunk Back between the Cab Sides, atop the Trunk Base and flush with the back edge of the frame. Place the Trunk Lid over the Trunk Back, butted against the rear Seat Back. Mark this position on the Seat Back. Attach the 7-inch piano hinge to the Trunk Lid and to the marked position on the Seat Back.

Building the Front Axle Assembly

1. The front axle support assembly is made by laminating alternating layers of pine and plywood. A scale drawing is provided in **Figure P**. Enlarge the drawing to make a full-sized paper pattern and cut five Axle Support pieces: two from ¾-inch pine and three from plywood.

2. Stack and glue the five Axle Support pieces, alternating layers, as shown in **Figure Q**. Clamp this assembly while the glue dries.

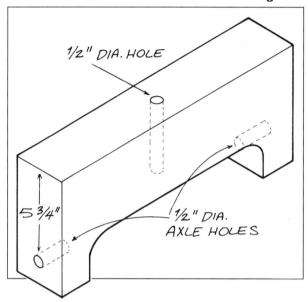

1/2" DIA. HOLE

5 3/4"

1/2" DIA. AXLE HOLES

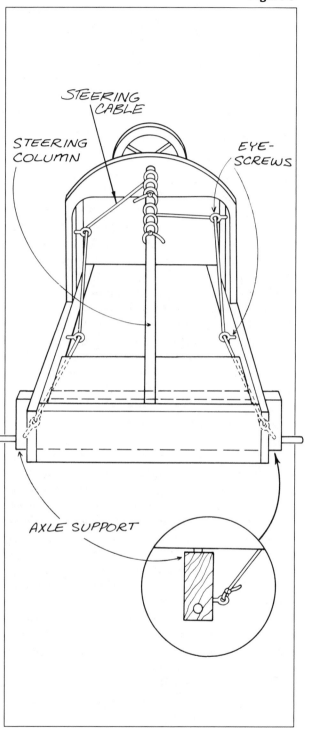

STEERING CABLE

STEERING COLUMN

EYE-SCREWS

AXLE SUPPORT

3. Three holes are drilled through the axle support assembly: one from the top to bottom to accommodate the machine bolt, and one through each of the lower extensions to accommodate the front axle (**Figure R**). Drill a ½-inch-diameter axle hole from end to end through each lower extension of the assembly, being careful to align them so the axle will fit. The ½-inch-diameter bolt hole should be drilled straight down through the center of the assembly.

4. Lubricate the 4½-inch-long machine bolt and insert it into the hole in the axle assembly, from bottom to top. Add a flat washer and then insert the end of the bolt up through the hole in the Platform that is attached to the car frame. Add another flat washer and the spring lock washer. Install the nut, leaving it loose enough to allow the axle assembly to swivel.

5. Insert the metal axle through the axle holes in the support assembly, leaving equal extensions on each side. At each end install a washer, a wheel, and another washer. Secure the wheel by inserting a cotter pin through the hole near the end of the axle.

Steering Assembly

Steering is accomplished by means of a simple cord-and-pulley arrangement that connects the Steering Column to the front axle assembly (**Figure S**).

1. A 24-inch length of 1-inch-diameter wooden dowel serves as the Steering Column. Cut the Column and round off the edge at one end. This will be the lower end. Drill a ¼-inch-diameter hole through the diameter of the Column, 7½ inches from the blunt upper end. This hole will accommodate the steering cord.

2. The steering wheel assembly is attached to the upper end of the Column as shown in **Figure S**. The Steering Ring is a 7-inch-diameter circle cut from ¾-inch pine, with a 5-inch-diameter circle cut out of the center. A scale drawing for the Ring is provided in **Figure F**. Cut the Ring, and cut four 2½-inch-long Spokes from ¼-inch-diameter wooden dowel rod.

3. Drill four evenly-spaced sockets into the Column, to accommodate the Spokes. Drill four holes through the Steering Ring, spacing them so they will line up with the sockets in the Column. Assemble the Steering Ring, Spokes, and Steering Column as shown in **Figure T**.

4. When the Steering Column is in place, the lower end is housed in a shallow socket. Insert the lower end of the Column through the hole in the Dashboard until it rests against the Platform and Front Spacer. Make sure the Column is straight, and not tilted sideways. Drill a shallow socket into the Platform-to-Spacer joint at the point where the end of the Column rests. Lubricate the end of the Column and the socket.

5. Two eyescrews guide the steering cable to each side of the axle support, as shown in **Figure S**. Install the eyebolts as shown in **Figure S**. Cut the plastic covered cable in half, so that you have two 3-foot lengths. Tie one end of each length to the eyescrew on each end of the axle support, as shown in **Figure S**. Thread each cable up through the eyescrew guides, as shown. Position the front wheels so that the towncar rolls straight forward. Wrap the right-hand-wheel cable counter-clockwise around the Steering Column, starting near the upper end and working down, as shown. Pull the cable taut, and insert a screw with a flat washer over the end of the cable to secure it to the Steering Column. Attach the left-hand-wheel cable to the Steering Column in the same manner, wrapping it clockwise.

Fitting the Pedals

Now you can "fit" the Pedal Bars to the Towncar driver. Have your child sit in the seat. The Pedals will

Figure T

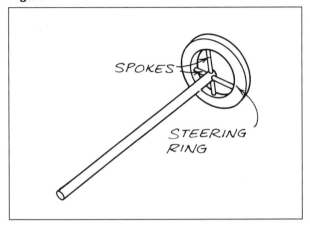

be attached to the Pedal Bars as shown in **Figure J**. Cut off the top of the Pedal Bars, if necessary, to make them a more comfortable length. Then trim the back upper corner of each Bar to accommodate the Pedal. Glue a Pedal to each Bar and secure the joints with screws. Cut four small triangular glue blocks to strengthen the Pedal-to-Pedal Bar joints.

Painting and Upholstering

Sand the entire assembly to remove any sharp edges and to prevent splintering. Paint with a non-toxic paint and allow to dry throughly before upholstering the seats. The seat covers consist of fiberfill padding and vinyl or any heavy material for the upholstery.

1. Cut two pieces of material or vinyl, each measuring 24 x 20 inches.

2. Place one of the pieces of material face down on a flat surface and center an appropriate amount of fiberfill over it. Fold the 24-inch sides of the material back over the fiberfill.

3. Position the seat cover in the seat with the open (unfolded) ends at the top and bottom.

4. Fold the top of the seat cover under and tack the material to the top of the Seat Back using the upholstery tacks. Repeat this at the bottom of the seat cover, tacking the material to the front edge of the Seat.

5. At the point where the Seat and the Seat Back meet, press home a few more tacks to keep the seat cover in place. Repeat steps 2 through 5 to upholster the remaining seat.

Dump Truck - page 7

Double Duty Wagon - page 22

Old-Fashioned Rocking Horse - page 26

Pumpmobile - page 31

Horsey Trike - page 38

Fire Engine - page 55

Towncar - page 44

Magical Unicorn - page 71

Easy Rockers - page 64

The Flying Steed - page 78

Folk Art Rocking Horse - page 83

Wheelbarrow - page 91

Spaceship - page 99

Tractor - page 115

Fire Engine

Ask any little guy what he wants to be when he grows up and you've got a better than even chance he'll say, "a fireman." After all, who else gets to wear a great hat, play in the water, and drive about town in a spiffy red truck. You may even discover that your future firefighter wears pigtails and bows, and prefers the term "fireperson!"

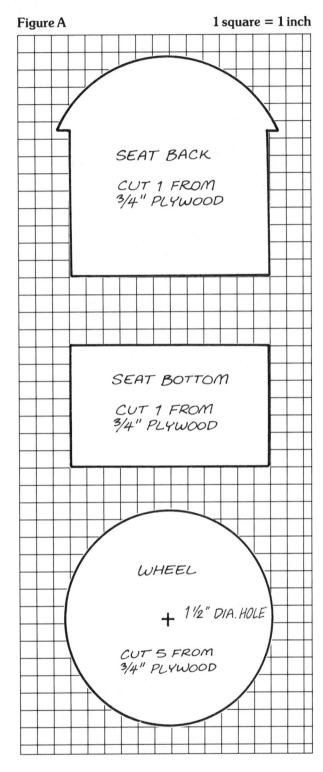

SEAT BACK

CUT 1 FROM
3/4" PLYWOOD

SEAT BOTTOM

CUT 1 FROM
3/4" PLYWOOD

WHEEL

+ 1½" DIA. HOLE

CUT 5 FROM
3/4" PLYWOOD

Materials

Exterior plywood: 4 x 8-foot sheet of ¾-inch; 1 x 4-foot piece of ½-inch.

Clear pine lumber: 12-inch length of 2 x 8-inch; 4-foot length of 2 x 4-inch; 8-foot length of 1 x 12-inch; 6-foot length of 1 x 2-inch.

Wooden dowel rod: 6-foot length of 1¼-inch diameter; two 4-foot lengths of ¾-inch diameter; two 3-foot lengths of ½-inch diameter.

Bolt: ½-inch diameter, 6½ inches long, with a nut and three washers.

Two small eyebolts, each about 1 inch long, with ¼-inch diameter eyes.

Flathead wood screws: ⅝ and 1½-inches long.

Box of 1½-inch long finishing nails; 2 small swivel pulleys; wood filler; carpenter's wood glue; carbon paper; kraft paper; and lubricant.

Non-toxic paint in the colors of your choice. We used red for the body, and white and black for the trim.

8-foot length of ⅛-inch-diameter nylon cord.

Several empty bleach bottles or other plastic containers to be cut into washers.

Cutting the Pieces

1. Refer to the scale drawings in **Figure A** (pages 56-60), and make full-size kraft paper patterns (see Tips & Techniques). Some additional parts, not shown in **Figure A**, will be cut as they are needed in the assembly process.

2. Cut the pieces according to the quantities and materials specified on the scale drawings. Label each piece. Drill all the holes, which are marked for position and proper diameter in **Figure A**. To cut the two large Body Sides, we suggest that you temporarily nail two pieces of plywood together. Draw the outline, and cut out both pieces at once. Drill the Rear Axle hole through both pieces before removing the holding nails.

3. Cut ten Dowel Pins, each 6½ inches long, from the ½-inch diameter dowel rod.

Assembly

You might read through the assembly instructions to get a bird's-eye view of the project before you begin work. Use glue and nails for all assembly steps, except where otherwise specified. Holding on to your hat is helpful, but not required.

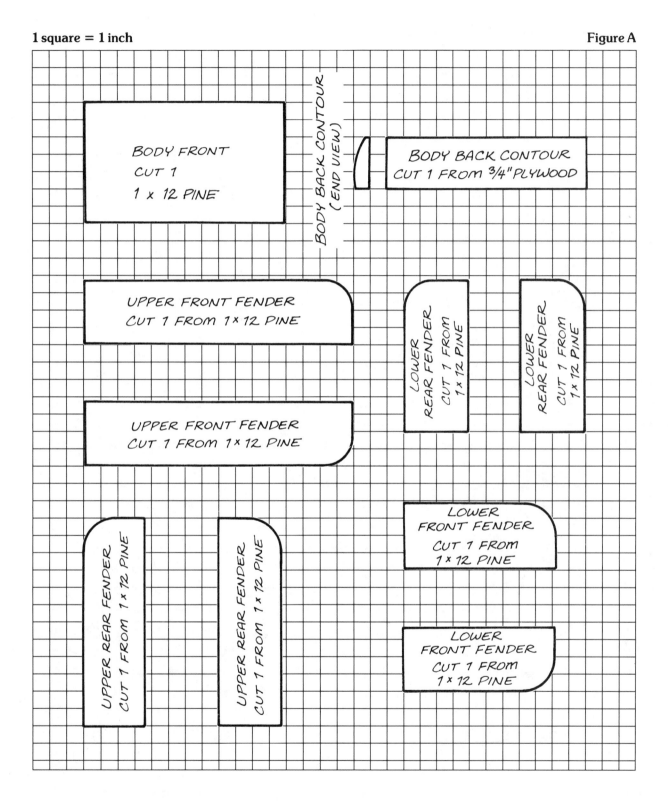

BODY FRONT
CUT 1
1 x 12 PINE

BODY BACK CONTOUR
(END VIEW)

BODY BACK CONTOUR
CUT 1 FROM 3/4" PLYWOOD

UPPER FRONT FENDER
CUT 1 FROM 1 x 12 PINE

LOWER
REAR FENDER
CUT 1 FROM
1 x 12 PINE

LOWER
REAR FENDER
CUT 1 FROM
1 x 12 PINE

UPPER FRONT FENDER
CUT 1 FROM 1 x 12 PINE

LOWER
FRONT FENDER
CUT 1 FROM
1 x 12 PINE

UPPER REAR FENDER
CUT 1 FROM 1 x 12 PINE

UPPER REAR FENDER
CUT 1 FROM 1 x 12 PINE

LOWER
FRONT FENDER
CUT 1 FROM
1 x 12 PINE

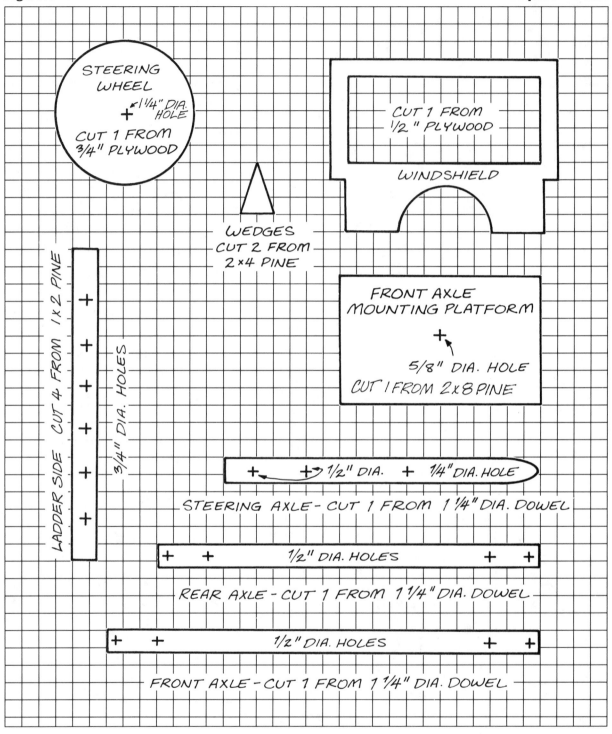

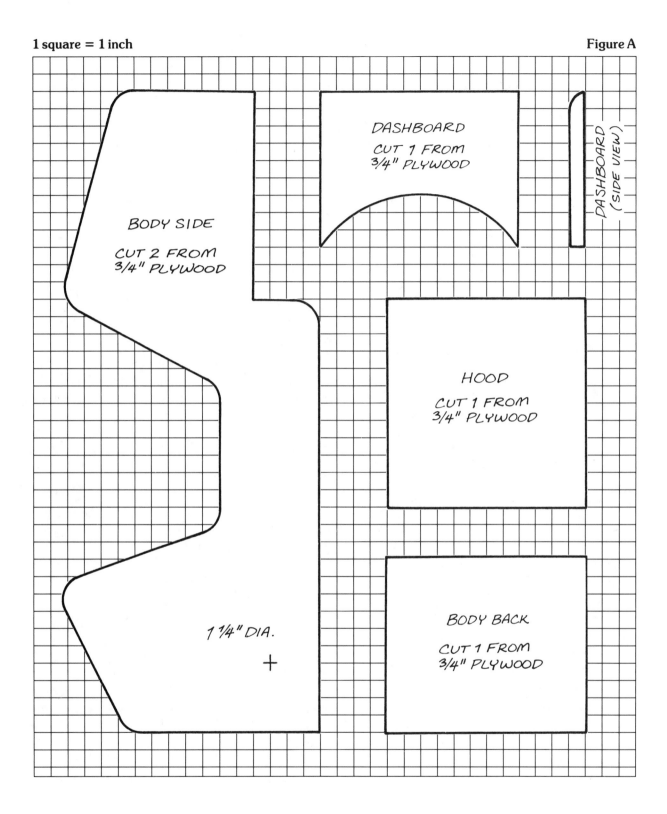

BODY SIDE

CUT 2 FROM
3/4" PLYWOOD

DASHBOARD

CUT 1 FROM
3/4" PLYWOOD

DASHBOARD
(SIDE VIEW)

HOOD

CUT 1 FROM
3/4" PLYWOOD

1 1/4" DIA.

+

BODY BACK

CUT 1 FROM
3/4" PLYWOOD

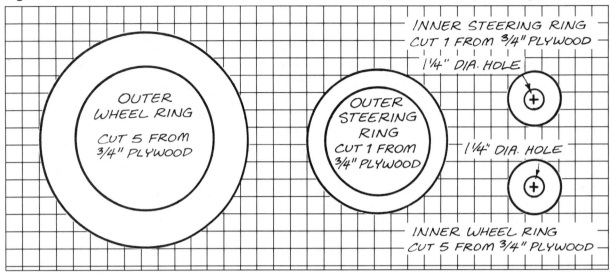

Figure A — INNER STEERING RING CUT 1 FROM 3/4" PLYWOOD, 1¼" DIA. HOLE; OUTER WHEEL RING CUT 5 FROM 3/4" PLYWOOD; OUTER STEERING RING CUT 1 FROM 3/4" PLYWOOD; 1¼" DIA. HOLE; INNER WHEEL RING CUT 5 FROM 3/4" PLYWOOD

Figure B

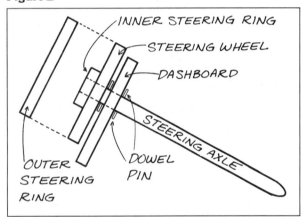

Figure B — INNER STEERING RING, STEERING WHEEL, DASHBOARD, STEERING AXLE, DOWEL PIN, OUTER STEERING RING

Figure C

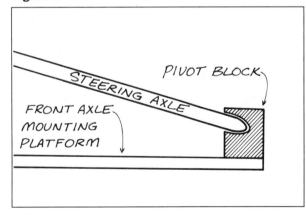

Figure C — PIVOT BLOCK, STEERING AXLE, FRONT AXLE MOUNTING PLATFORM

Steering Wheel and Axle

1. Insert the Steering Axle through the hole in the center of the Dashboard (**Figure B**). The Dashboard fits between the two holes at the blunt end of the Steering Axle. Glue a Dowel Pin in each of the holes, as shown in the illustration, but do not glue the Steering Axle to the Dashboard. Sand the rounded end of the Steering Axle smooth.

2. Apply glue liberally, and fit the Steering Wheel over the blunt end of the Steering Axle, letting the wheel sit flush against the Dowel Pin (**Figure B**). Place the Inner Steering Ring over the end of the Steering Axle. Cut or sand the blunt end of the Steering Axle even with the Inner Ring. Attach the Outer Steering Ring to the Steering Wheel and finish the open grain.

3. Attach the two Wedges to the back of the Dashboard, referring to **Figure D** for placement.

4. Cut a 2½-inch length of the pine 2 x 4 for the Pivot Block. Attach the Pivot Block to the Front Axle Mounting Platform, as shown in **Figure D**, using glue and the longer wood screws. Drill a 1½-inch diameter socket into the Pivot Block. This socket will receive the rounded tip of the Steering Axle, and should be drilled at an angle (**Figure C**). Sand the socket smooth, and apply lubricant liberally inside the socket and at the tip of the Steering Axle, to produce "power steering."

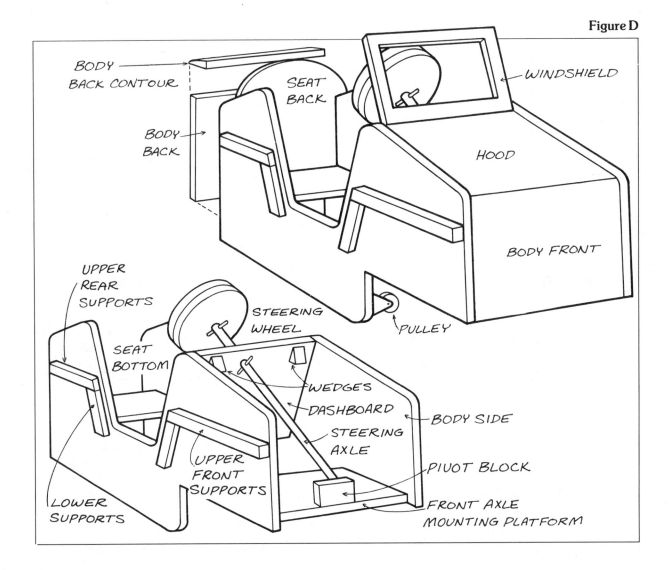

Body Assembly

1. Cut the following Fender Supports from the pine 1 x 2: two Upper Front Supports, 1½ x 13 inches; two Upper Rear Supports, 1½ x 9 inches; and four Lower Supports, 1½ x 8 inches. Attach these to each Body Side piece (**Figure D**).

2. Refer to **Figure D** as you position and glue the main body parts: Begin with the Body Sides, Seat Bottom, Dashboard (including the Steering assembly), and Front Axle Mounting Platform. Be sure that the lower end of the Steering Axle fits into the socket. It may be necessary to enlarge or adjust the angle of the socket to get a proper fit. Drive a few nails to hold the parts in place.

3. Refer to **Figure D** and add the Seat Back, Body Back Contour, Body Back, Windshield (set at an angle on the Wedges), Hood, and Front. Drive a few more holding nails, and pull the sides of the Fire Engine together with the pipe clamps. Finish nailing all parts in place, recess the nails, and let the glue dry for 24 hours.

4. Install the pulleys, using glue and the shorter screws (refer to **Figure D**).

Figure E

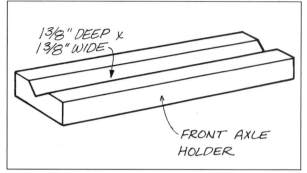

1⅜" DEEP x 1⅜" WIDE

FRONT AXLE HOLDER

Figure F

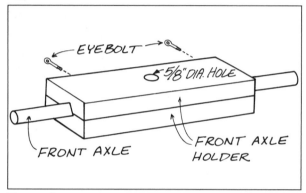

EYEBOLT

5⅝" DIA. HOLE

FRONT AXLE

FRONT AXLE HOLDER

Figure G

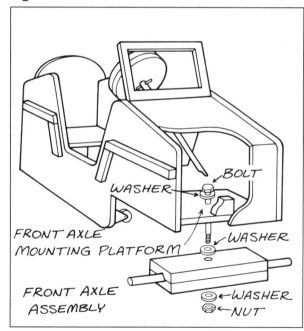

BOLT

WASHER

FRONT AXLE MOUNTING PLATFORM

WASHER

FRONT AXLE ASSEMBLY

WASHER

NUT

Figure H

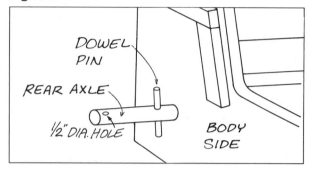

DOWEL PIN

REAR AXLE

½" DIA. HOLE

BODY SIDE

Front Axle Assembly

1. Cut two Front Axle Holders, each 17½ inches long, from the pine 2 x 4. Using the circular saw, cut a V-shaped groove down the center of each, as shown in **Figure E**.

2. Sandwich the Front Axle between the two Front Axle Holders, so that the ends of the axle extend equally (**Figure F**). Glue and nail the three pieces together, install the eyebolts, and drill a ⅝-inch diameter hole through the exact center of the entire axle assembly as shown.

3. Lubricate the Bolt and insert it through the Front Axle Mounting Platform and the front axle assembly, placing the three washers and nut as shown in **Figure G**. This Bolt serves as a pivot for the front axle, and should be left loose enough to allow the assembly to swivel freely.

Rear Axle and Wheels

1. Refer to **Figure H**, and glue the Rear Axle in place, making sure that it extends evenly on both sides of the body. Glue a Dowel Pin into the hole closest to the body on each end of the axle.

2. To assemble a wheel (you'll need five – one will be a "spare"), glue and nail the Outer and Inner Wheel Rings to the Wheel, aligning the center holes and rims.

3. Lubricate the inside of the hole and the end of the axle. Cut eight circular washers from the empty bleach bottles, each 3 inches in diameter, with a 1½-inch diameter center hole. Install the wheel on the axle, adding a plastic washer on each side of the wheel. Glue a Dowel Pin through the remaining hole in the axle. Repeat for the remaining wheels.

Figure I

Trim

1. Cut the following trim pieces from the pine 1 x 12: one Upper Grille, 1½ x 15 inches; two Lower Grilles, 1½ x 13½ inches; and six circular Lights, each 3½ inches in diameter. Use what's left of the 1¼-inch diameter dowel rod for the Hood Ornament.

2. Attach the Upper and Lower, Front and Rear Fenders to the Body Sides over the corresponding Fender Supports. The Spare Wheel goes on the back, and Upper and Lower Grilles on the front. Glue two of the circles together for each Headlight, and attach to the Upper Grille. Taillights (the remaining two circles) go at the lower corners of the Body Back. Place the Hood Ornament at the front of the Hood, or in the mouth of your most vocal critic.

Finishing Work

1. Round off the Body Front and Body Back with a rasp, and sand flush with the sides and top.

2. Sand the entire Fire Engine, to eliminate rough edges and splinters.

3. Thread the nylon cord through the remaining hole in the Steering Axle (yes, it is now behind the Dashboard, but not difficult to get at), leaving equal amounts of cord on each side of the hole. Wrap one end of the cord clockwise around the Steering Axle four or five times, then thread it through the left-hand pulley, and attach it to the eyebolt on the left side of the front axle assembly. Do the same with the other end of the cord, wrapping it counter-clockwise around the Steering Axle, passing it through the right-hand pulley, and tying it to the right-hand eyebolt.

4. Paint the Fire Engine red, with black and white trim, or in other colors of your choice.

Ladders

1. Cut twelve Rungs, each 7 inches long, from the ¾-inch diameter dowel rod.

2. Glue the Rungs into the Ladder Side Pieces (which you already cut and drilled according to the scale drawings, and put aside where you could easily find them – right?) Let the glue dry overnight.

3. Paint the ladders. When they are dry, nail them to the sides of the Fire Engine, as shown in **Figure I**.

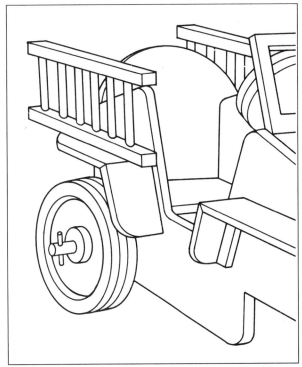

Figure J

ENGINE NO.44

Signs

1. Cut two rectangles, each 4 x 8 inches, from the pine 1 x 12. Sand, and paint them white.

2. Full-size letter patterns are provided in **Figure J**. Use carbon paper to transfer the letter outlines to the dry sign boards. Paint the letters.

Fill the Fire Engine with kid power (an abundant, easy-to-find fuel), sit back, and enjoy the hoopla.

Easy Rockers –
Eli Lion and Austin Elephant

Who says horses are the only animals given to rocking? These 9 x 30 x 30-inch critters are so easy to build, you'll want to bag a whole menagerie. The animals you are about to build are true. Only the heads can change – to inspire the safari-bent.

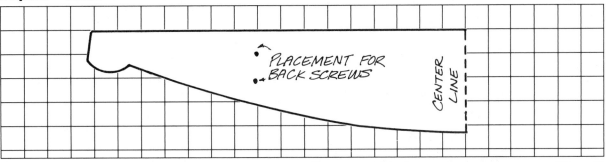

Materials

For each body:

5 linear feet of pine 1 x 6.

6 linear feet of pine 2 x 6.

4 linear feet of pine 2 x 8.

Eight No. 6 gauge flathead wood screws, 2 inches long.

Two No. 6 gauge flathead wood screws, 3 inches long.

4d finishing nails.

180-foot roll of brown 3-ply jute for the tail.

Wood glue, wood filler, and a wood finish such as stain or non-toxic paint.

For the lion head:

16 linear inches of pine 2 x 12.

11-inch length of 1-inch-diameter wooden dowel rod.

540-foot roll of brown 3-ply jute for the mane.

A small amount of non-toxic black acrylic paint and a small paint brush.

For the elephant head:

30 x 48-inch piece of ½-inch-thick interior plywood.

Four No. 6 gauge flathead wood screws, 2 inches long.

A small amount of non-toxic black acrylic paint and a small paint brush.

Cutting the Pieces

1. A scale drawing for the Rocker is provided in **Figure A**. Enlarge the drawing and transfer it to a length of 2 x 6. Cut one Rocker, and drill two ⅛-inch-diameter holes through it, 7¼ inches from the back end, as indicated on the drawing. In addition, drill two holes of the same diameter 9½ inches from the front end of the Rocker. Use this Rocker as a guide to cut and drill a second one, so they will be identical and the holes will be

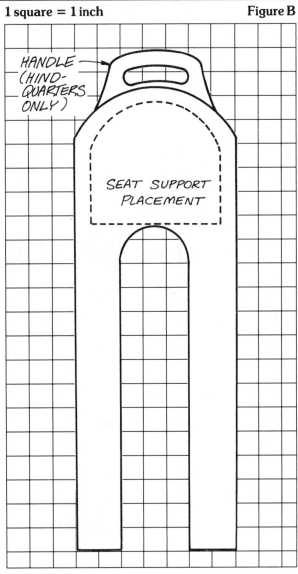

Figure C

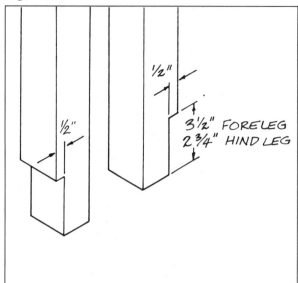

Figure D

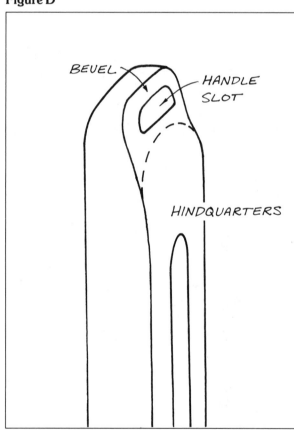

Figure E   1 square = 1 inch

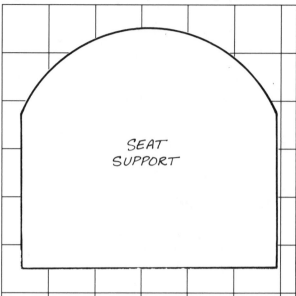

perfectly aligned. Enlarge the holes on one side of each Rocker so you can countersink the screw heads.

2. A scale drawing for the Fore- and Hindquarters is provided in **Figure B**. The two pieces are basically identical, except the Hindquarters has a small extension at the upper end to accommodate a handle slot. Enlarge the drawing and cut one of each piece from 2 x 8. Cut a ½ x 3½-inch notch along the outer edge of each foreleg, as shown in **Figure C**. In addition, cut a ½ x 2¾-inch notch along the outer edge of each hind leg. Cut out the handle slot in the Hindquarters where indicated on the drawing, and bevel one side of the handle extension at a slight angle (**Figure D**).

3. A scale drawing for the Seat Support is provided in **Figure E**. Enlarge the drawing and cut two Supports from 1 x 6.

4. The seat consists of seventeen slats, each ¾ x ¾ x 14 inches. Rip these slats from 1 x 6.

5. A scale drawing for the Lion Head is provided in **Figure F**. Cut one Lion head from 2 x 12. For the handle, drill a 1-inch-diameter hole through the head where indicated on the drawing. For the mane, drill thirty ¼-inch-diameter holes through the head at the points indicated on the drawing.

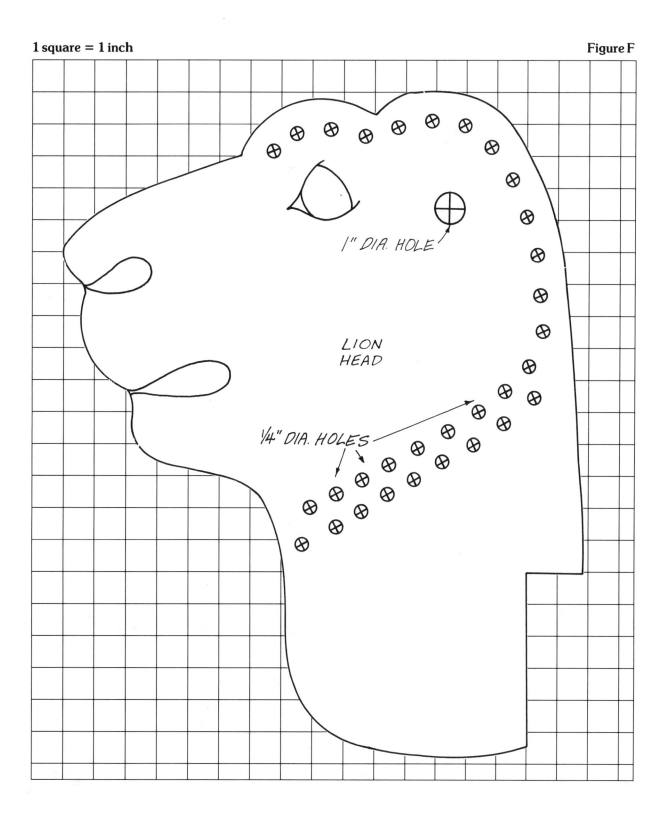

1" DIA. HOLE

LION
HEAD

1/4" DIA. HOLES

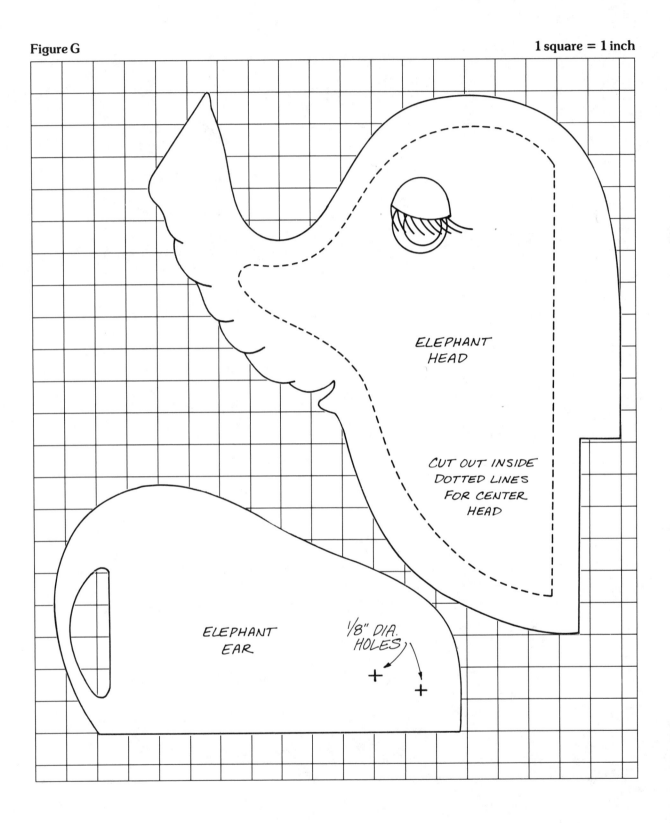

ELEPHANT
HEAD

CUT OUT INSIDE
DOTTED LINES
FOR CENTER
HEAD

ELEPHANT
EAR

1/8" DIA.
HOLES

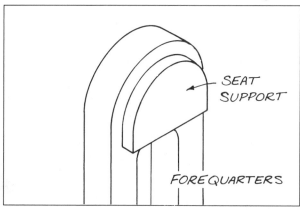

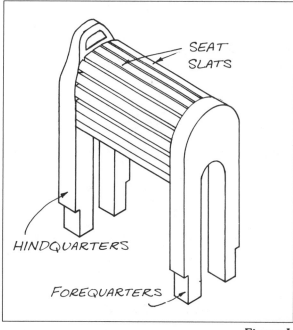

6. Scale drawings for the Elephant Head and Ear are provided in **Figure G**. Enlarge the drawings and cut three Elephant Heads and two Ears from ½-inch plywood. Drill two ⅛-inch-diameter holes through each Ear where indicated on the drawing. Enlarge the holes on one side so you can countersink a screw head. To make the assembled head lightweight, cut out the center portion of one of the head pieces along the dotted lines on the drawing.

Assembling the Body

1. Glue and nail one Seat Support to the upper end of the Forequarters, so that there is a ¾-inch space between the curved upper edges of the pieces, as shown in **Figure H**. Attach the remaining Seat Support to the upper end of the Hindquarters in the same manner (**Figure H**).

2. The Seat Slats are connected between the forequarters and hindquarters, as shown in **Figure I**. To begin, glue and nail one slat at the top of the curved edge of the Seat Supports, as shown. Attach eight slats on each side of the center slat, butting the lower corners along the curve, as shown. Butt the last three slats side by side with no gaps between them. Countersink the nail heads and cover them with wood filler.

3. Attach the assembled body to the Rockers as shown in **Figure J**. Align the ends of the foreleg and hind leg on each side with the screw holes in the Rockers, as shown. Insert two screws through the Rocker into each leg, and plug the screw holes.

Figure J

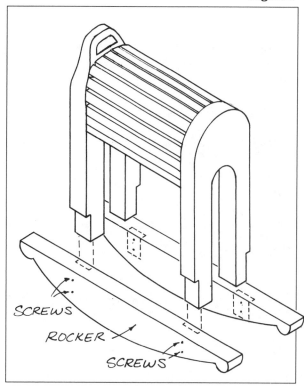

Figure K

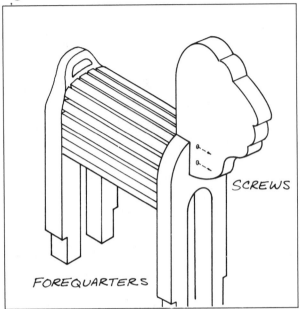

SCREWS

FOREQUARTERS

Figure M

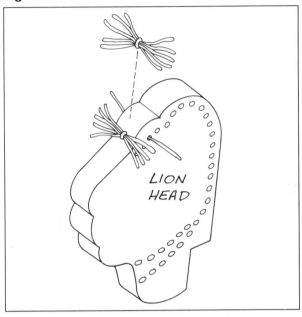

LION
HEAD

Figure L

EAR

Adding the Head

1. Attach the head of your choice to the upper end of the Forequarters, as shown in **Figure K**. Use glue and two 3-inch screws inserted through the forequarters into the head.

2. For the Lion, insert the dowel Handle into the hole in the head, leaving equal extensions on each side, and glue securely in place.

3. For the Elephant, attach one Ear on each side, using glue and screws, as shown in **Figure L**.

Finishing

1. Stain or paint the animal. Use black paint and a small brush to paint the eyes, nose, and mouth. Allow the paint to dry.

2. To make the tail, cut forty-eight lengths of jute, each 30 inches long. Insert the length of wire into the holes in the Hindquarters and twist the ends together under the seat. Thread one end of each length through the wire loop, and pull until the ends are even. Tie a short length around the strands, 1½ inches from the top. Divide the jute into three sections, each with sixteen strands. Braid the three sections together, tie a length around the tail about 4 inches from the end, and unwind the ends.

3. The lion's mane consists of bundles of jute each tied to the head through a hole, as shown in **Figure M**. To make one bundle, cut twenty lengths of jute each 6 inches long, and tie them together in the middle with another length. Thread one length of the bundle through one hole in the head and tie the ends together securely. Repeat this procedure for each hole.

The Magical Unicorn

Legend states that the unicorn can be seen, as a true unicorn, only by children and those who are pure of heart. To the believer, the unicorn is a beast of mystical beauty with a soul of pure joy. You'll believe the legend too when you see the look in your smallest tyke's eyes as they first catch sight of this magical riding toy. Made with love, there's a little more to this unicorn than just wood and paint. The unicorn lives – believe.

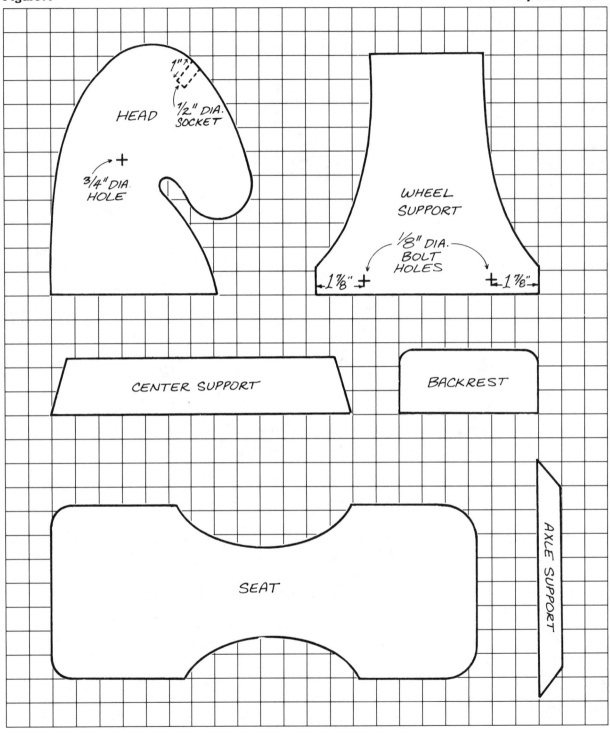

HEAD

1"

½" DIA.
SOCKET

¾" DIA.
HOLE

WHEEL
SUPPORT

⅛" DIA.
BOLT
HOLES

1⅞"

1⅞"

CENTER SUPPORT

BACKREST

SEAT

AXLE SUPPORT

Materials

Wooden dowel rod: 36-inch length of ¾-inch diameter; 3-inch length of ½-inch diameter; 8-inch length of ¼-inch diameter.

6-foot length of 1 x 12-inch pine lumber (includes 2-foot length for wooden wheels).

Four wheels, each 5 inches in diameter, with a ⅞-inch-diameter center hole. You can use replacement lawn mower wheels, or cut wooden wheels from the 1 x 12 listed above.

4 x 8-inch piece of ¼-inch waferwood or plywood.

Four metal bolts, each 1¾ inches long, with washers and nuts to fit.

Handful of 4d finishing nails.

Fourteen small-gauge flathead wood screws, each 1¾ inches long.

Sandpaper, wood glue, kraft paper, beeswax or hard soap, and wood filler.

6 x 8-inch piece of white leather, fabric, or vinyl to be used for the Horn.

Small amount (handful) of fiberfill.

8-inch length of seam binding tape.

20-foot length of decorative white twisted cord to be used for the Mane.

Cutting the Pieces

To make your job easier (which is no mean feat, considering the simplicity of this project), we suggest that you sand the whole length of the pine board before you start drawing and cutting the pieces. Sand first with medium sandpaper and finish with fine.

1. Scale drawings for the pattern pieces are provided in **Figure A**. There are six pattern pieces: Head, Wheel Support, Center Support, Seat, Axle Support, and Backrest. Enlarge the drawings to make full-size paper patterns (see Tips & Techniques).

2. Draw the outline of each piece on the pine 1 x 12, following the suggested cutting layout in **Figure B**.

3. Cut two Wheel Supports, two Axle Supports, and one each of the remaining pieces. If you have chosen wooden wheels, cut eight 5-inch-diameter wheels and drill a ⅞-inch-diameter center hole through each.

4. Cut two Axles, each 14½ inches long, from the ¾-inch dowel rod. The remainder will be the Handle.

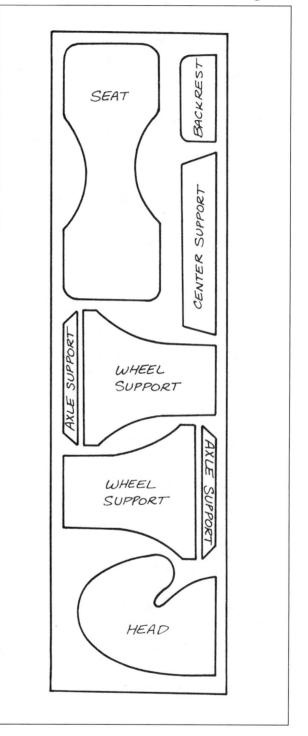

Figure B

Figure C

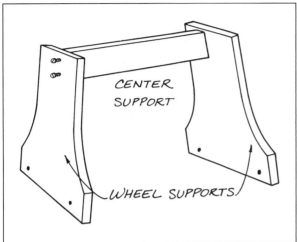

Figure D

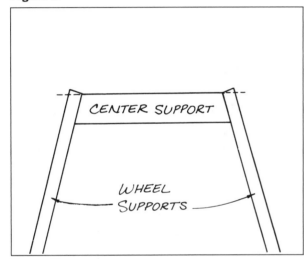

Figure E

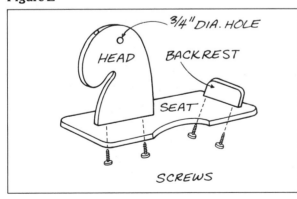

5. Drill a ¾-inch-diameter hole through the Head where indicated on the scale drawing. This hole will accommodate the dowel-rod handle, which will be added later. Drill a ½-inch-diameter socket, 1 inch deep, into the upper front edge of the Head piece where indicated on the scale drawing to accommodate the ½-inch-diameter Horn dowel. Drill two holes through each of the Wheel Supports where indicated on the scale drawing, using a drill bit that is slightly larger than the diameter of the bolt shanks. Use the same bit to drill a hole 4⅛ inches from each end of each Axle. Drill an additional ¼-inch-diameter hole ¼ inch from each end of each Axle piece.

6. Round off the edges of the Seat, the curved sides of the Wheel Supports, the top and sides of the Backrest, and all edges of the Head, excluding the straight bottom edge. You can accomplish this with sandpaper, or use a router with a quarter-round bit.

7. Cut eight Washers from waferwood or plywood. Each Washer should be a 2-inch-diameter circle with a ¾-inch-diameter center hole.

Assembly

Use wood screws for all assembly operations, except where nails are specified. Use glue with both nails and screws. To avoid cracking the wood be sure to pre-drill all screw holes.

1. Carefully center each of the Wheel Supports against one end of the Center Support as shown in **Figure C**. Fasten the pieces with two screws on each side.

2. Notice that the outer corner of each Wheel Support extends above the top of the Center Support (**Figure D**). Bevel the upper edge of each Wheel Support so that they are flush with the Center Support.

3. Bevel the lower edge of the Backrest at approximately the same angle as used to trim the Wheel Supports. The exact angle is not important, as long as it allows the Backrest to tilt slightly to the rear of the Unicorn when attached to the Seat.

4. Position the Head and Backrest on the Seat (**Figure E**). Use two screws to secure each piece, as shown. Be sure to angle the screws that go into the Backrest. (Screws not inserted at the proper angle will produce complaints from the rider that will be heard throughout the entire neighborhood.)

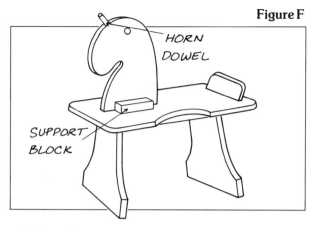

HORN
DOWEL

SUPPORT
BLOCK

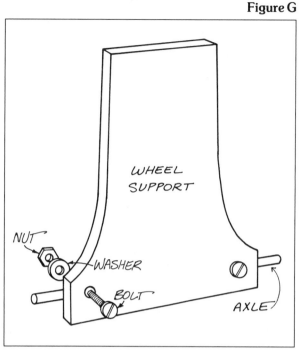

WHEEL
SUPPORT

NUT

WASHER

BOLT

AXLE

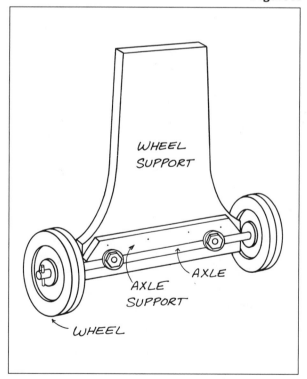

WHEEL
SUPPORT

AXLE

AXLE
SUPPORT

AXLE

WHEEL

5. To add extra reinforcement to the sides of the Head, cut two wooden Support Blocks, each ¾ x 6 inches, from the remaining pine scraps. Fasten them to either side of the Head and Seat using glue and small finishing nails.

6. Glue the 3-inch length of ½-inch wooden dowel into the socket drilled in the upper edge of the Head. This dowel forms the base for the Unicorn's fabric horn which will be attached after painting.

7. Carefully center the top assembly (Head, Seat, and Backrest) over the support assembly (Wheel Supports and Center Support) as shown in **Figure F**. Glue them together, and drive two nails through the top of the Seat into each of the Wheel Supports. You may use screws for extra stability. Recess the nails (or countersink the screws) and fill the holes with wood filler.

Adding the Wheels

1. Insert the bolts through the holes in the Wheel Supports and then through the Axles. Secure each bolt with a washer and nut (**Figure G**).

2. Glue the eight Wheel pieces together in pairs to create four wheels, each 1½ inches thick. When glueing, place the Wheels so that the grain of one is perpendicular to the grain of its mate.

3. Lubricate the ends of the Axles and the center holes of the wheels, using beeswax or hard soap. Slip a Wheel over each Axle end, placing a washer on each side. Secure with a 2-inch length of ¼-inch-diameter dowel rod (**Figure H**).

4. Nail and glue the Axle Supports to the Wheel Supports, over the Axles, as shown in **Figure H**.

Figure I

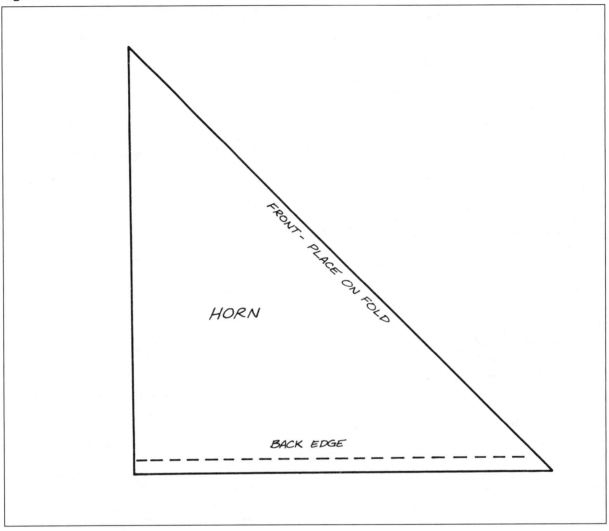

HORN

FRONT - PLACE ON FOLD

BACK EDGE

Painting the Unicorn

Unicorns are always of the purest white, so unless you feel the need for a unicorn-of-a-different-color, white for the unicorn and black for the wheels and facial detail should do it. Of course, you can get as creative as your little heart desires (a pink unicorn with blue eyes might be unique).

Be careful not to allow the paint to freeze the wheels, and allow the paint to dry throughly before proceeding with the fabric Horn.

The Unicorn's Horn

The Unicorn's Horn is simply a fabric cone stuffed with fiberfill and attached over the ½-inch dowel rod mounted on the unicorn's head. Now is the time to dust off the old creative brain cells – the fancier the unicorn's horn, the better.

1. Use the pattern provided in **Figure I** to cut one Horn piece from the fabric.

2. Fold the piece in half, placing right sides together,

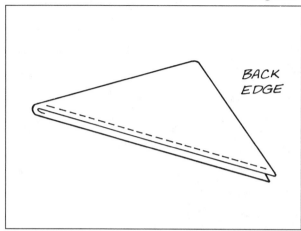

BACK EDGE

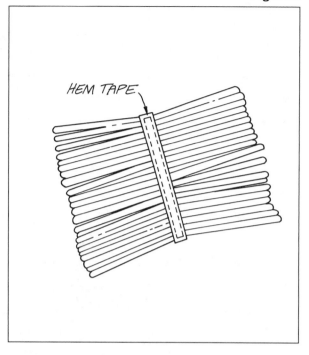

HEM TAPE

and stitch a ½-inch-wide seam along one edge (**Figure J**). Press the seam open. Press a ½-inch-wide hem to the wrong side of the fabric completed around the continuous back edge.

3. Turn the cone right side out, and glue a spiraling strand of bright ribbon around the cone.

4. Stuff a small amount of fiberfill into the tip of the cone. Place the fabric cone over the wooden dowel on the head of the unicorn with the seam at the top. Stuff as much fiberfill as possible into the cone, around the wooden dowel. Glue the Horn to the Head, around the lower edge.

5. Insert the Handle and glue in place.

The Mane

The unicorn's glistening white mane is made from twenty 12-inch lengths of ⅜-inch-diameter decorative white twisted cord.

1. Cut the cord into twenty 12-inch lengths.

2. Stitch each piece of cord to the 8-inch length of hem tape so that equal lengths hang from either side (refer to **Figure K**).

3. Starting at the base of the horn, glue the hem tape (with the cord over) along the center back edge of the unicorn's head (**Figure L**).

When finished, you will see a little wooden riding toy like the one pictured on the first page. What your children will see will be something entirely different – watch the reflections in their eyes, and see the Unicorn.

Figure L

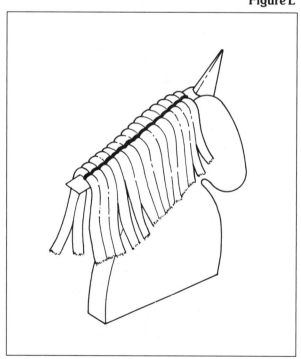

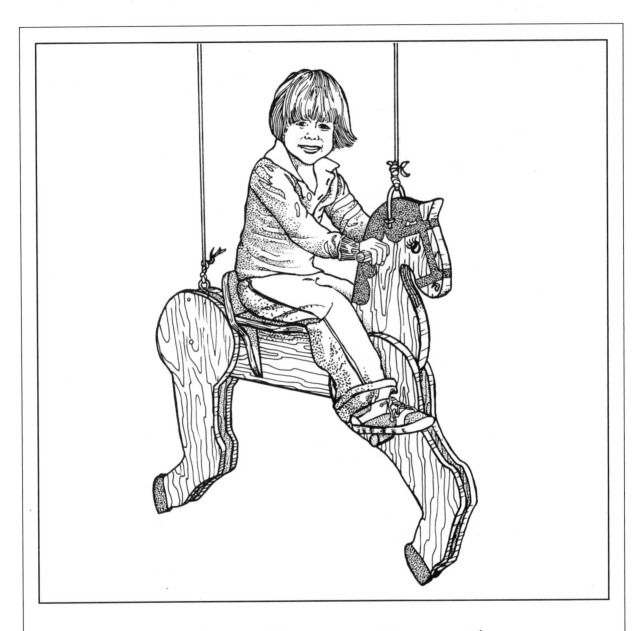

The Flying Steed

Leap on this high-stepping steed and swing into the sunset! The legs and head of this kid-powered plywood pony pivot so even a 3-year-old can swing it himself. Overall dimensions: 8 x 36 x 42 inches.

Materials

4 x 4-foot square piece of ¾-inch exterior-grade plywood or waferwood.

3 linear feet of 2 x 8 pine.

12-inch length of ½-inch-diameter wooden dowel rod.

20-inch length of 1-inch-diameter wooden dowel rod.

Three ⅜-inch-diameter carriage bolts, each 3½ inches long, with six flat washers, three lock washers, three hex nuts, and three cap nuts.

One heavy-duty U-bolt, 2 inches wide, with crossbar and nuts.

Two No. 6 gauge flathead wood screws, each 1 inch long, and a few 2d finishing nails.

Approximately 50 feet of heavy nylon ski rope to hang the swing. (Be sure to choose rope that's rated to handle well above the weight it will need to hold.)

Waterproof glue, exterior wood stain, exterior wood sealer, and small amounts of brown, black, and white exterior paints.

Cutting the Pieces

1. Scale drawings for all the horse pieces are provided in **Figure C**. Enlarge the drawings and cut two Heads, four Legs, one Saddle, and one Saddle Back from plywood. In addition, cut one Body from 2 x 8.

2. Cut two Spacers from 2 x 8, each 2 x 2 inches.

3. The Head, Legs, and Body must be drilled to accommodate the bolts and various dowels. Drill each hole where indicated on the drawings in **Figure C**. Glue together the two Head pieces and drill two ½-inch-diameter holes and one 1-inch-diameter hole where indicated. Cut a rectangular slot near the top of the Head, to accommodate the U-bolt crossbar. Two of the Leg pieces will serve as forelegs, and the remaining two will be hind legs. Drill the four holes indicated in each foreleg, and the two holes indicated in each hind leg.

4. Bevel the back edge of the Saddle at a 10-degree angle, as shown in **Figure A**.

Assembly

1. Glue a Spacer to one foreleg and one hind leg, as shown in **Figure B**.

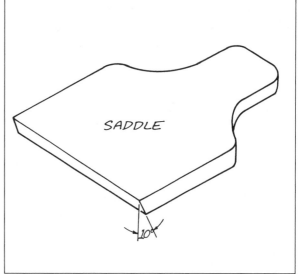

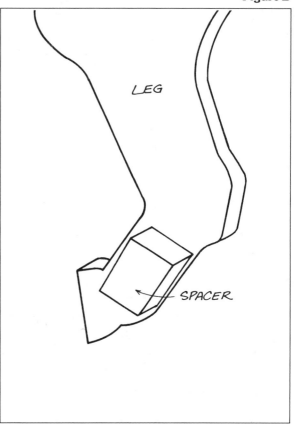

Figure C   **1 square = 1 inch**

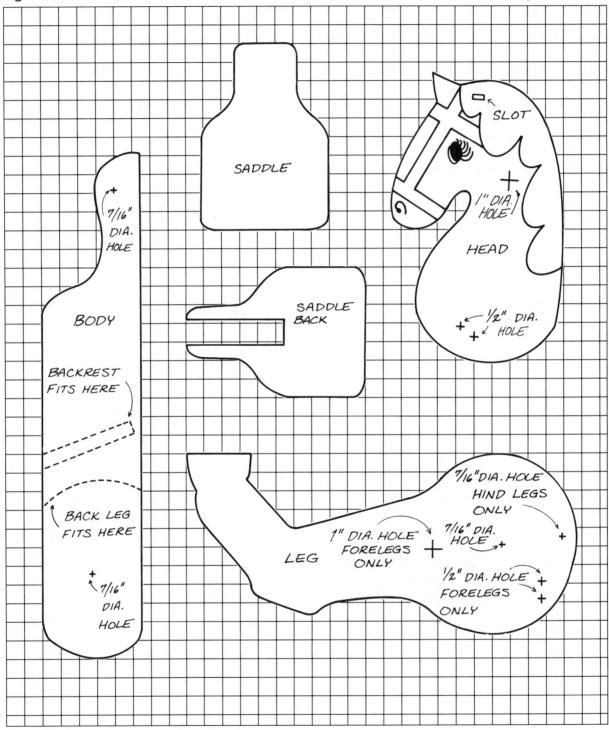

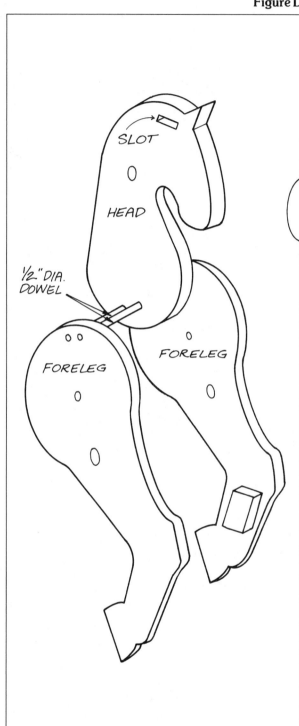

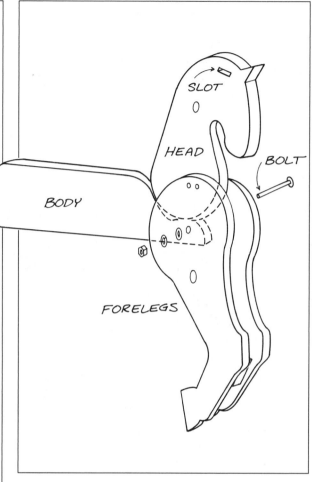

2. The Head and forelegs are assembled as shown in **Figure D**. Use glue and a length of ½-inch-diameter dowel inserted through the holes in each piece to secure the assembly.

3. The Head-and-forelegs assembly pivots on a carriage bolt inserted through holes in the forelegs and Body, as shown in **Figure E**. Insert the bolt through one foreleg, add a washer, then push the bolt through the Body hole. Add another washer on the opposite side the of the Body, push the bolt through the opposite foreleg, and add a washer and a lock washer before you screw on the hex nut. Tighten the nut, but not so much that it prevents the Head and forelegs from moving on the Body. Screw the cap nut over the end of the bolt.

Figure F

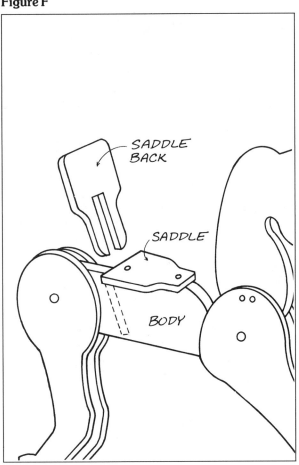

SADDLE BACK

SADDLE

BODY

Figure G

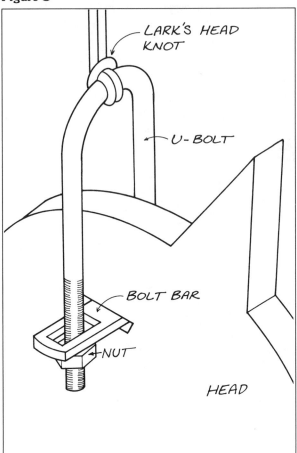

LARK'S HEAD KNOT

U-BOLT

BOLT BAR

NUT

HEAD

4. Attach the hind legs to the rear end of the Body in the same manner as you did the Head and forelegs.

5. Attach the Saddle to the upper edge of the Body using glue and screws inserted down through the Saddle, as shown in **Figure F**. Countersink the screws and cover the heads with plugs or wood filler. Glue the Saddle Back to the Body immediately behind the Saddle, and nail it to the back edge of the Saddle.

6. Cut the 1-inch-diameter dowel in half so that you have two 10-inch lengths. Insert one length through the Head hole, leaving equal extensions on each side, and glue it in place. Insert and glue the remaining length through the foreleg holes in the same manner.

7. To attach the U-bolt to the top of the head, insert the bolt bar through the slot and fasten the U-bolt

to it with nuts. To provide a rope attachment at the back of the horse, insert a carriage bolt through the remaining holes in the hind legs and add a washer, lock washer, hex nut, and cap nut.

Finishing

1. Stain or paint the horse. We stained it first, then painted a black mane and hooves, brown saddle and reins, and big brown eyes. Finish the horse with a coat of waterproofing sealer.

2. Hang the horse swing in a shady spot using ski rope attached to the U-bolt in front and the carriage bolt in back. Be sure to use knots that will not slip, such as the Lark's Head knot shown in **Figure G**.

Folk Art Rocking Horse

Almost too pretty to ride! This little filly is a charmer in a child's room, and can kick up some conversation in a den. Once you have the pieces cut, the assembly is as easy as falling off a horse. Overall dimensions: 14 x 29 x 41 inches.

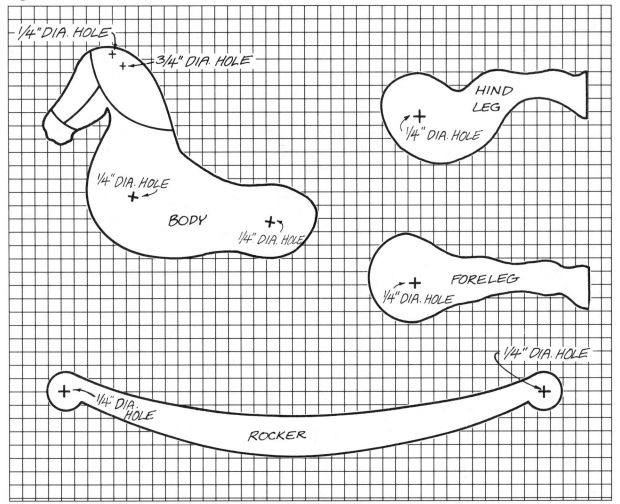

Materials

8 linear inches of pine 1 x 4.

16 linear feet of pine 2 x 10.

2 linear feet of pine 2 x 16. This wood will be used for the horse's body. If your lumberyard can't supply this size of wood, you can edge-glue two narrower boards, clamp them until completely dry, and then cut the Body piece.

1 linear foot of ¼-inch-diameter wooden dowel rod.

1 linear inch of ½-inch-diameter wooden dowel rod.

7 linear inches of ¾-inch-diameter wooden dowel rod.

27 linear inches of 1-inch-diameter wooden dowel rod.

One spherical wooden drawer pull, 1½ inches in diameter, for the saddle horn.

Twenty yards of white three-strand drapery tieback rope, for the mane and tail.

1 x 7-inch piece of white felt.

Electrical tape.

Seventeen No. 6 gauge flathead wood screws: nine 2 inches long, and eight 3 inches long.

No. 18 wire brads, each 1½ inches long.

Carpenter's wood glue, sealer, acrylic paints (we used peach, cherry, kelly green, dusty rose, purple, and white), and watercolor paint (we used teal blue).

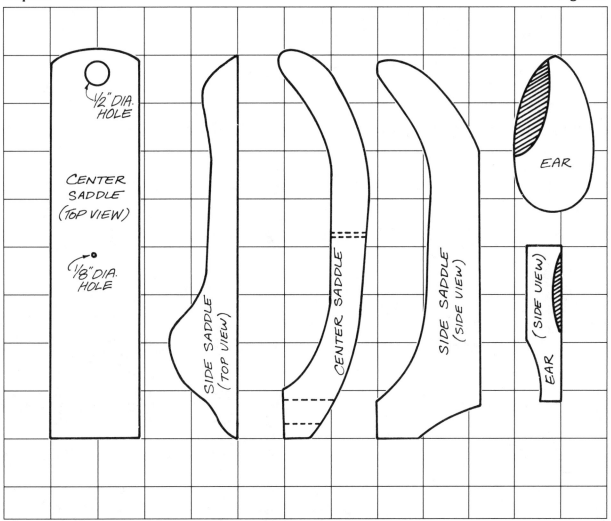

Cutting the Pieces

1. Scale drawings for the Body, Foreleg, Hind Leg, and Rocker are provided in **Figure A**. Scale drawings for the Ear and Saddle are provided in **Figure B**. Enlarge the drawings to make full-size paper patterns.

2. Cut the following pieces from 2 x 10: two Forelegs, two Hind Legs, and two Rockers. Cut one Body from 2 x 16, or from two narrower edge-glued boards.

3. Cut one Center Saddle from the remaining 2 x 10, using the top view pattern (**Figure B**). Cut the contours using the side view pattern. Cut two Side Saddles from 2 x 10 using the top view pattern. Cut the contours on each piece using the side view pattern.

4. Cut four Leg Supports from the remaining 2 x 10, each 2¼ x 3½ inches.

5. Cut two Ears from 1 x 4, using the side view pattern (**Figure B**). Use the front view pattern to contour the inner side of each Ear. The shaded areas on the drawing indicate portions that will be shaped later.

6. Cut the 1-inch-diameter dowel rod in half so that you have two 13½-inch-long Tie Rods.

7. Several of the pieces need to be shaped before

Figure C

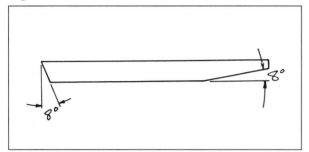

Figure D

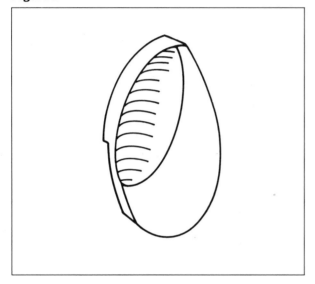

Figure E

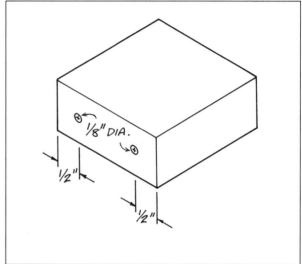

you assemble the horse. (It's always something!) Because each leg slants in two directions (sideways and either forward or backward), you have some beveling and mitering to do. On one Foreleg, bevel the inner side (not the end) at an 8-degree angle, beginning 5½ inches from the rounded upper end, as shown in **Figure C**. On the same leg, cut an 8-degree compound miter (don't panic – read on) across the lower end as shown. To cut a compound miter, simply cut diagonally across the end from corner to corner, instead of straight across from side to side as you would for a simple miter. In this case, the miter should be widest at the inside back corner of the leg, and narrowest at the outside front corner. Cut the same bevel and miter on the other Foreleg, but be sure to cut so that the legs are mirror images of each other.

8. Cut a similar bevel and miter on each Hind Leg. At the lower end, the compound miter should be widest at the inside front corner and narrowest at the outside back corner. Make the Hind Legs mirror images.

9. Use a chisel to create a spoon-shaped indentation on the outside front edge of each Ear, where indicated by the shaded area on the scale drawing (**Figure B**). A correctly-shaped ear is shown in **Figure D**. Be sure that the finished ears are mirror images of each other.

10. You just have a little drilling to do, and you'll be ready to start the assembly process. Drill the holes through the Rockers, Legs, Body, and Saddle where indicated on the scale drawing, using the specified drill bit sizes. For the saddle horn, drill a ½-inch-diameter socket in the Center Saddle where indicated on the drawing (**Figure B**). In addition, drill a ½-inch-diameter socket into the spherical wooden drawer pull. Drill two ⅛-inch-diameter holes through each Leg Support, each ½ inch from the edge, as shown in **Figure E**.

Assembly

The horse and rocker base are assembled separately and then joined and finished. Begin by temporarily assembling the horse and the rocker base, then adjust the legs and leg supports before securing the joints with glue and screws.

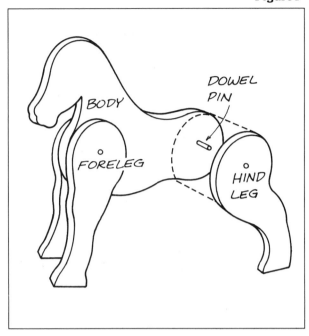

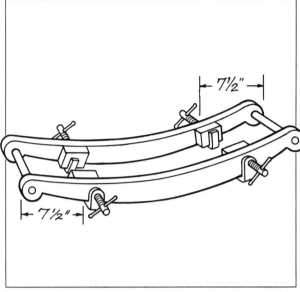

1. The assembled horse is shown in **Figure F**. To begin, insert a 4-inch length of ¼-inch-diameter dowel through the hole in the forequarters of the Body and hang a Foreleg on each side of the Body, placing the beveled side of each leg against the body as shown. Attach the hind legs in the same manner.

2. The rocker base consists of Rockers, Leg Supports, and Tie Rods. To assemble the base, align the Rockers side by side, about 10 inches apart. Insert the ends of the Tie Rods into the aligned Rocker holes, as shown in **Figure G**. The ends of the rods should be flush with the outer sides of the rockers, as shown. Glue the ends of the Tie Rods into the holes. Trim the ends if necessary.

3. Temporarily clamp one Leg Support approximately 7½ inches from one end of each Rocker, as shown in **Figure G**. Clamp another Support 7½ inches from the opposite end of each Rocker.

4. Place the assembled horse on the base, with the fore- and hind legs centered on their Leg Supports. Adjust the supports and the legs until each hoof sits flat on its support at the front and back of the rockers (**Figure H**). When you have adjusted the legs correctly, glue

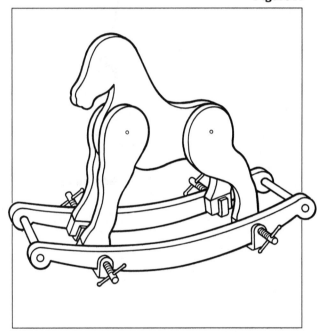

them in place on the Body. Secure each Support in the proper position by inserting a 3-inch screw through each hole into the Rocker. In addition, insert a 2-inch screw up through each Support into the leg.

Figure I

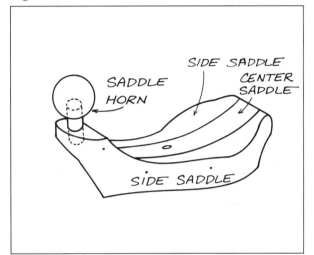

Figure J

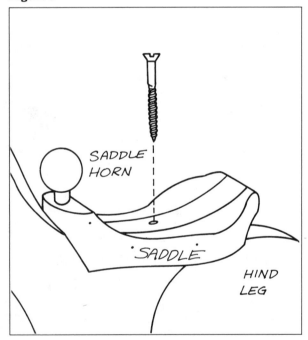

Figure K

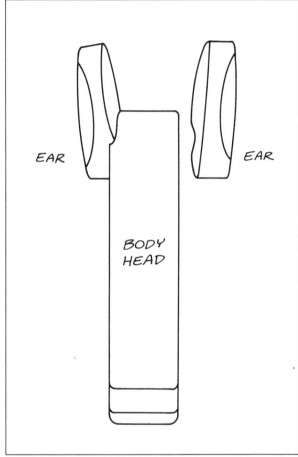

5. The assembled saddle is shown in **Figure I**. To begin, attach a Side Saddle to one side of the Center Saddle aligning the contours as shown. Secure the joint with glue and brads inserted through the Side Saddle into the Center Saddle. Attach the remaining Side Saddle to the opposite side of the Center Saddle in the same manner. To make the saddle horn, insert one end of the length of ½-inch-diameter dowel into the socket in the saddle. Glue the spherical wooden drawer pull on the opposite end of the dowel.

6. Position the assembled saddle on the horse Body just in front of the hind legs, as shown in **Figure J**. To secure it, insert a screw down through the saddle hole into the Body.

7. To attach the ears, cut a 4-inch length of ¼-inch-diameter dowel and insert it through the Body head hole, leaving equal extensions on both sides. Attach an Ear on each side of the head, as shown in **Figure K**.

8. The length of ¾-inch-diameter dowel will serve as a handle. Insert it into the remaining head hole, leaving equal extensions on each side, and glue in place.

Figure L

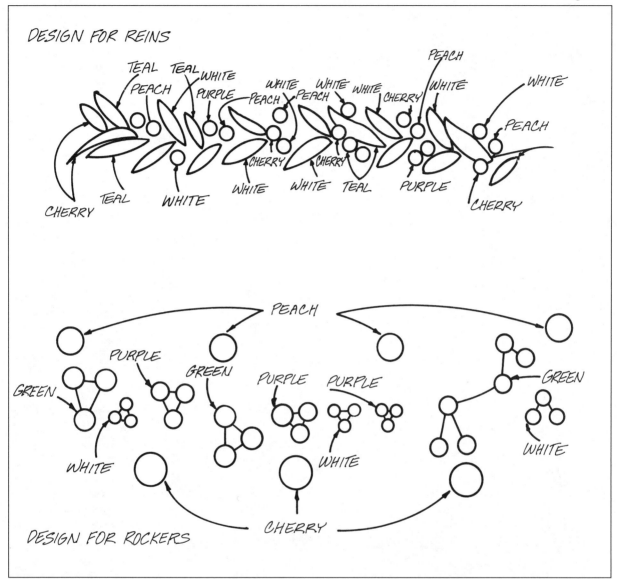

DESIGN FOR REINS

DESIGN FOR ROCKERS

Finishing Details

1. Use a wood rasp to round off the edge of the haunch on each leg. Carefully sand the entire horse, eliminating all sharp corners and edges.

2. Paint or stain and seal the horse. We finished the horse with a decorator touch by first white-washing it (to make a whitewash, mix equal amounts of white paint and water). We also coated the base and saddle with a wash made of teal blue watercolor paint, and painted a design on top of it, using peach, purple, cherry, white, and kelly green paints. The design consists of small dots arranged in a pattern as shown in **Figure L**. To paint the design, dab the tip of a small paintbrush on the wood to make each dot. Paint the reins on the horse body using the same colors.

Figure M

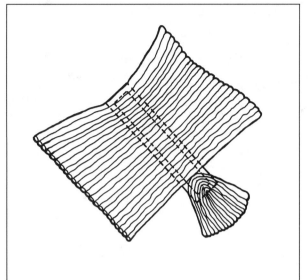

Figure O

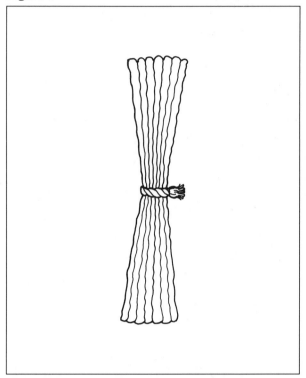

Figure N

3. For the mane and tail, cut the drapery tieback rope in half, so that you have two 10-yard lengths. To make the mane, cut one rope into 10-inch lengths. Place the lengths side by side along the felt strip, as shown in **Figure M**, and stitch them to the strip. Glue the mane along the upper edge of the horse's head directly behind the ears, as shown in **Figure N**. Trim the mane on both sides and near the back end as shown. To create the forelock, pull several strands of the mane forward and trim them to about 3 inches long. Unravel the ends.

4. To make the tail, cut the remaining rope into 18-inch lengths. Place the lengths together and twist a short length of wire around the middle, as shown in **Figure O**. Tie an additional length of rope around the wire, and secure the ends by wrapping electrical tape around them, as shown. Drill a ½-inch-diameter socket in the horse body, approximately 1½ inches behind the saddle. Glue the taped end of the rope into the socket in the upper edge of the horse's body, behind the saddle. Unravel the ends as you did for the mane.

Wheelbarrow

After building every conceivable four- and three-wheeled riding machine, we were contemplating the safety of a unicycle when someone remembered the sheer fun of being pushed in a wheelbarrow. This smooth-riding model features a removable seat for times when more domestic chores are at hand. Overall dimensions: 20 x 26 x 60 inches.

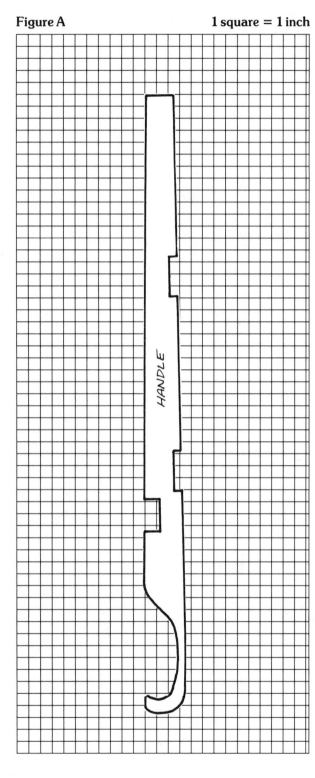

HANDLE

Materials

28 linear feet of rot-resistant pressure-treated pine 1 x 10 lumber.

18 x 27-inch piece of ¾-inch exterior plywood.

8 linear feet of rot-resistant treated pine 2 x 4.

9 linear inches of rot-resistant treated pine 4 x 4.

1-foot length of ½-inch-diameter wooden dowel rod.

12-inch length of ½-inch-diameter steel rod, threaded on both ends, with two 2-inch-diameter flat washers, two lock washers, two 1⅜-inch-diameter flat washers, and two hex nuts.

52-inch strip of thin rubber, 1½ inches wide. You can cut this from an old inner tube.

No. 6 gauge flathead wood screws, each 1 inch long.

Waterproof glue, wood stain and sealer or paint.

Cutting the Pieces

1. Each handle consists of two pieces that are glued together. The inner piece is notched to accommodate the Floor Supports and Legs. For a good match, we nailed two lengths of 1 x 10 together temporarily, and cut two Handle pieces simultaneously. A scale drawing for the Handle is provided in **Figure A**. Enlarge the drawing and cut two Handles from 1 x 10, but do not cut the notches at this time; cut the sides straight. Use one of these Handles as a guide to cut a second pair.

2. Select one Handle from each pair to be the inner piece, and temporarily nail them together. Cut out the floor support and leg notches where indicated on the drawing (**Figure A**). The front end of each inner Handle piece must be beveled to accommodate the wheel hub. Take the pieces apart and bevel the front end of each at a 5-degree angle, as shown in **Figure B**.

3. Cut the pieces listed here from 1 x 10. **Note:** Some of the pieces are wider than the stock, so you'll have to spline two pieces together, and then cut to the specified dimensions.

Description	Quantity	Dimensions
Sideboard	2	8 x 28 inches
Headboard	1	14¼ x 18 inches
Seat	1	5 x 18 inches
Front Support	1	3½ x 13¼ inches
Rear Support	1	3½ x 16 inches
Leg	2	2½ x 13½ inches

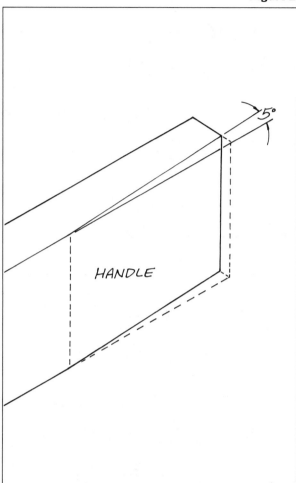

HANDLE

Figure C

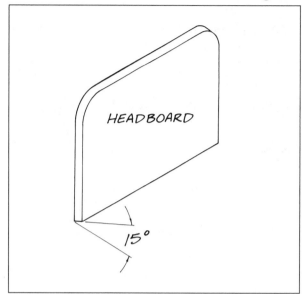

HEADBOARD

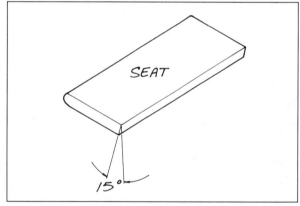

SEAT

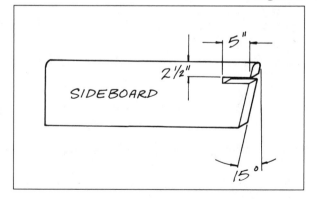

SIDEBOARD

4. Bevel one long edge of the Headboard at a 15-degree angle, as shown in **Figure C**. On the opposite long edge, round off the two corners of the Headboard, as shown. In addition, bevel one long edge of the Seat at a 15-degree angle, and round off the opposite long edge (**Figure D**).

5. Miter one end of each Sideboard at a 15-degree angle, as shown in **Figure E**. Round off one corner of the opposite short edge, as shown. In addition, each Sideboard must be notched to accommodate the Seat. Cut a 5-inch notch, ¾ inch wide into the mitered edge of each Sideboard, 2¼ inches from the longest edge, as shown in **Figure E**.

Figure F

Figure G

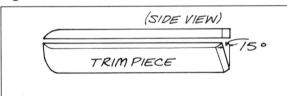

Figure H

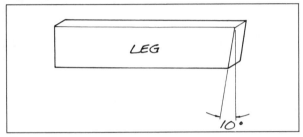

Figure I   1 square = 1 inch

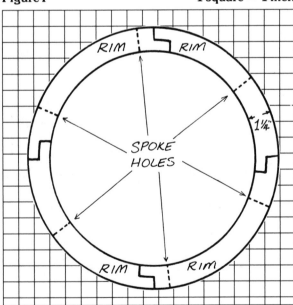

Figure J

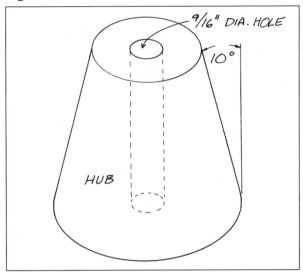

6. Miter both ends of the Front and Rear Supports at a 5-degree angle, as shown in **Figure F**. In addition, miter one end of each Leg at a 10-degree angle, as shown in **Figure G**.

7. For the side trim pieces, rip approximately 7 feet of 1 x 10 down to a 1¾-inch width. Cut two 25½-inch and two 13-inch lengths to serve as the trim pieces. Miter one end of each piece at a 15-degree angle, as shown in **Figure H**. In addition, round off the opposite end of each of the short Trim pieces, as shown.

8. The wheel consists of four interlocking Rim pieces, six Spokes, and three Hub pieces. A scale drawing for the Rim is provided in **Figure I**. Enlarge the drawing and cut four Rim pieces from 2 x 4. For the Spokes, rip approximately 3 feet of 2 x 4 down to a 1-inch width. Cut six Spokes, each 5¼ inches long. For the Hub, cut three lengths of pine 4 x 4, each 3 inches long.

9. Cut two of the Hub pieces into cone-shaped cylinders, as shown in **Figure J**. To begin, draw a 3-inch-diameter circle on one end of a Hub piece you cut earlier. Tilt the table on a bandsaw so that the blade cuts at a 10-degree angle, and cut around the circle. For the remaining (center) Hub, repeat the procedure with the bandsaw table level, to cut a regular cylinder. In addition, drill a 9/16-inch-diameter hole through the center of each of the three Hub pieces, as shown.

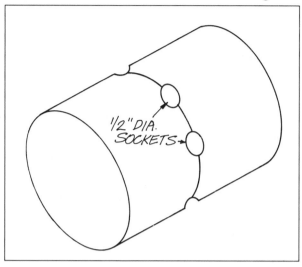

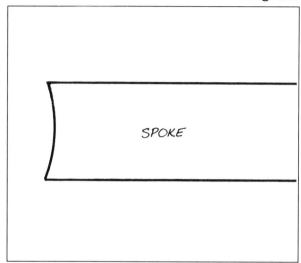

10. The Rim and Hub must be drilled to accommodate dowel pegs that support the ends of each Spoke, as shown in **Figure K**. Draw a line around the center of the cylindrical Hub. Drill six ½-inch-diameter sockets into the Hub, each one ½-inch deep, spacing them evenly around the line. Some of the Rim pieces have two Spoke holes, some have one. Drill a ½-inch-diameter hole through each Rim piece where indicated on the drawing (**Figure I**). In addition, cut six 1-inch pegs from ½-inch-diameter dowel, and six 1½-inch pegs.

11. The hub end of each Spoke must be rounded to fit snugly against the Hub. A full-size drawing of the Spoke end curve is provided in **Figure L**. Cut the curve in one end of each spoke, and be sure that all the finished Spokes are exactly the same length, or you'll end up with a cock-eyed wheel. In addition, drill a ½-inch-diameter socket centered in the both ends of each Spoke, ½ inch deep.

Assembling the Wheel

1. The assembled wheel is shown in **Figure M**. To begin, insert a ½-inch peg into the curved end of each Spoke and glue in place. Insert the peg of each Spoke into the drilled center Hub and glue in place, as shown.

2. To join the Rim pieces, insert a screw through the lap joint at the end of each piece, as shown in **Figure M**. Be sure to position the Rim pieces so that those with

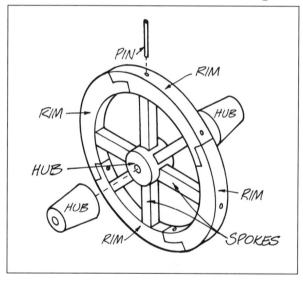

one spoke hole are on opposite sides of the circle, as shown. Place the assembled Rim around the spoked Hub, and align the Rim holes with the holes in the Spoke ends. Insert a 1½-inch pin through the Rim hole into the Spoke end, as shown, and secure with glue.

3. Glue one cone-shaped Hub to each end of the center Hub, aligning the axle hole in all three pieces, as shown in **Figure M**.

4. Glue the rubber strip around the wheel rim.

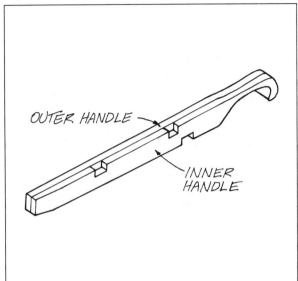

OUTER HANDLE

INNER HANDLE

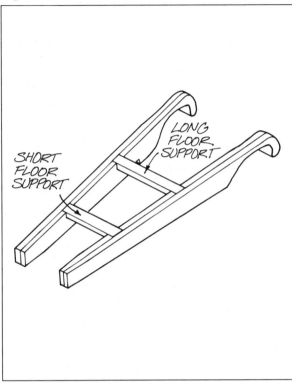

LONG FLOOR SUPPORT

SHORT FLOOR SUPPORT

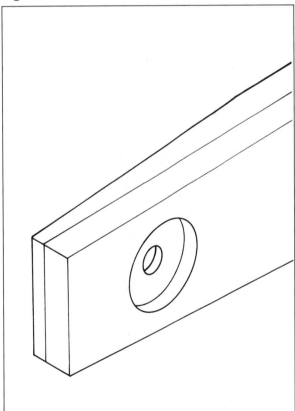

Assembling the Handles

1. Glue one notched inner Handle piece to an outer Handle piece, as shown in **Figure N**. Glue the remaining Handle pieces together in the same manner. After the glue is dry, round off the edges of each Handle grip.

2. Drill a ½-inch-diameter axle hole through the front end of each Handle, as shown in **Figure O**. The hole should be drilled at a 90-degree angle to the beveled inner side of the Handle, as shown. So you can recess the axle and nuts, drill a 1½-inch-diameter socket approximately ¼ inch deep into the outer side of each Handle, aligned with the axle hole, as shown.

3. Position the Handles so that the notched inner sides are facing each other. Install the short Floor Support, placing the ends in the Handle notches farthest from the curved handle grips, as shown in **Figure P**. Insert screws down through the Support into the Handle. Install the long Floor Support in the remaining notches in the same manner.

4. Insert the unmitered end of one Leg into the lower notch in one Handle, as shown in **Figure Q**. Insert screws through the Leg into the Handle. Install the remaining Leg on the other Handle in the same manner.

Assembling the Barrow

1. Assemble the Floor, Sideboards, and Headboard, butting the edges as shown in **Figure R**. The Floor covers the lower edges of the Side- and Headboards, and the Headboard covers the front edge of each Sideboard, as shown. Insert screws up through the Floor into the Side- and Headboards, and through the Headboard into the front edge of each Sideboard.

2. Slide the Seat through the slot in one Sideboard with the beveled edge against the Headboard, as shown in **Figure R**. Push the Seat through until the end engages in the slot on the opposite Sideboard.

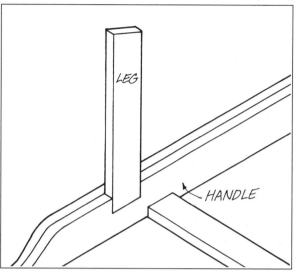

Figure Q

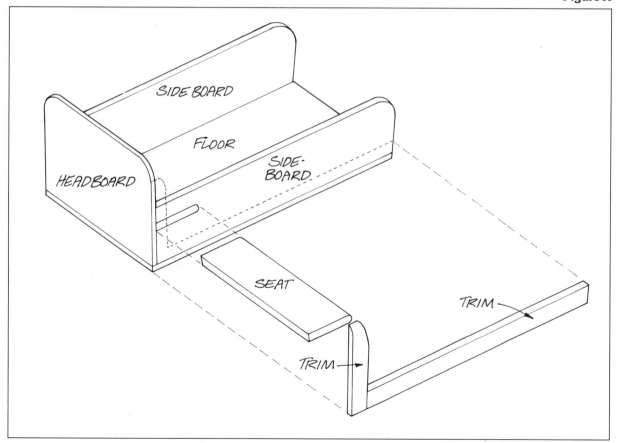

Figure R

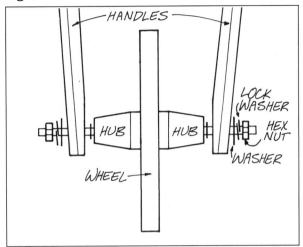

3. Attach one short Trim piece to one side edge of the Headboard, as shown in **Figure R**. Insert screws through the Trim into the Headboard, and plug the screw heads. Attach one long Trim piece along the side

edge of the Floor, as shown. Insert screws through the Trim into the Floor and Sideboard, and plug the screw heads. Attach the remaining Trim pieces to the opposite side of the barrow in the same manner.

Final Assembly

1. Position the wheel between the Handles, aligning the Hub holes, as shown in **Figure S**. Slide the metal axle through the hole in one Handle, add a small flat washer between the Handle and the Hub, then push the axle through the Hub. Add a small flat washer on the opposite end of the Hub, and push the axle through the opposite Handle. On each end of the axle, place a large flat washer, lock washer and hex nut.

2. Position the barrow on top of the handle assembly, as shown in **Figure T**. The front end of the barrow should be approximately 10¾ inches from the front end of the handle assembly. Insert screws up through each Floor Support into the barrow Floor.

3. Stain or paint the wheelbarrow, and finish with a coat of waterproofing sealer.

Figure T

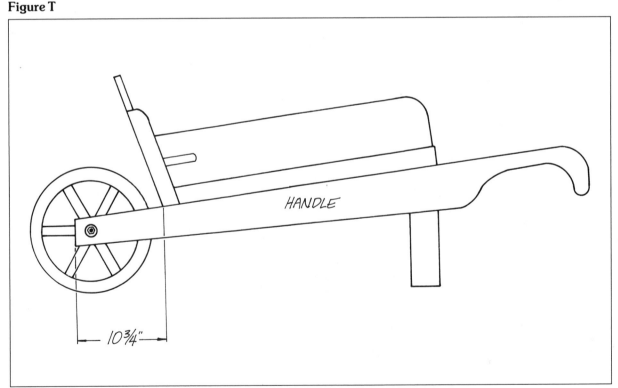

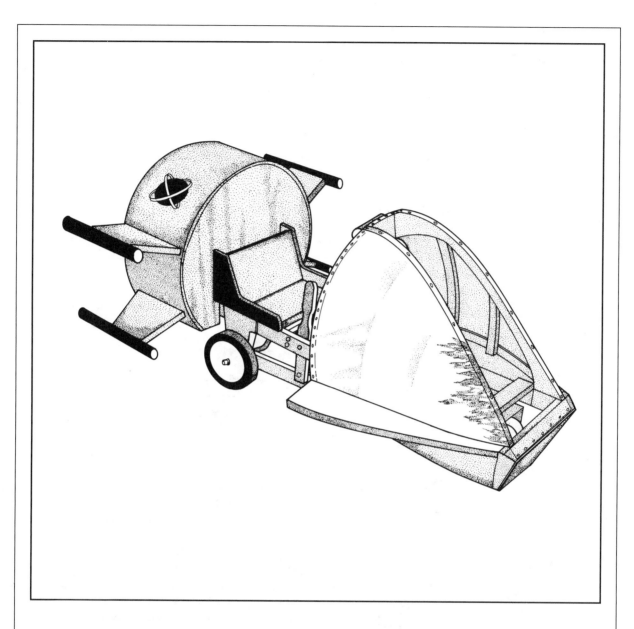

Spaceship

Beam me up, Scotty! Here's our answer to high-tech travel – it features a nose cone with plastic windshield, one-handed steering lever, a cargo bay, and rocket thrusters. Overall dimensions: 30 x 38 x 56 inches.

Figure A

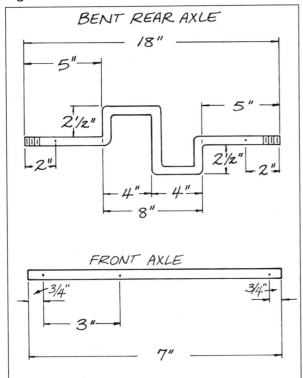

both rods must be drilled to accommodate cotter pins, as shown in **Figure A**. If your drill is not designed for this job, one of the shops listed above will be able to perform this task for you.

Two metal conduit clamps that will accommodate ½-inch-diameter pipe.

Five cotter pins.

Seven ⁵⁄₁₆-inch-diameter bolts, each 2 inches long, with two flat washers, a lock washer, and hex nut, all of which match the diameter of the bolt.

One 20d common nail.

Escutcheon nails, each 1 inch long.

No. 6 oval-head wood screws, each ½ inch long.

No. 6 flathead wood screws, each 1¼ inches long.

Carpenter's wood glue, silicone caulk or hot-melt glue and a glue gun.

Paint in your choice of colors. We used silver, orange/red, yellow, and black.

Building the Frame

The assembled frame is shown in **Figure B**. Refer to this diagram as you work through the steps in this section to aid you in assembly.

1. For the Rails, cut two 9 x 55-inch pieces from ¾-inch plywood. A scale drawing of the Rail is provided in **Figure C**. Enlarge the drawing to make a full-size paper pattern, and transfer the pattern to one of the lengths you cut earlier. So that both Rails will be identical, temporarily nail the boards together, and cut the Rails simultaneously. As indicated, drill a ½-inch-diameter axle hole through both Rails, 6½ inches from the upper edge, before you disassemble them.

2. The axle support portion of each Rail is reinforced with two Facers cut to match the rear portion of the Rail (**Figure D**). Cut four 6 x 8-inch Facers from ¼-inch plywood, and nail them together temporarily. Use the rear portion of one Rail as a pattern to cut the plywood Facers and drill the axle holes.

3. Glue and nail a Facer to each side of one Rail piece (**Figure D**). Attach the remaining Facers to the other Rail in the same manner.

4. Four Spacers serve to connect the two Rails. Cut four Spacers from ¾-inch plywood, each 2 x 10 inches.

Materials

2 x 5-foot piece of ⅛-inch plywood.

1 x 2-foot piece of ¼-inch plywood.

4 x 8-foot sheet of ¾-inch plywood.

5¼ linear inches of pine 4 x 4.

6 inches of ¾-inch-diameter wooden dowel rod.

6 feet of 1¼-inch-diameter wooden dowel rod.

12 x 30-inch piece of ⅛-inch clear thermoplastic.

46-inch length of ⅛ x 1-inch pine lattice.

30 linear inches of 1½-inch-diameter PVC pipe.

Three lawnmower wheels, each 8 inches in diameter and with ½-inch-diameter hub holes.

2 yards of heavy canvas.

Two ½-inch-diameter metal axle rods: one 7 inches long, and one 30 inches long. The long rod should be threaded on both ends, and it must be bent as shown in **Figure A**. If you're not confident about bending the rod yourself, ask for help at a hardware shop, metal shop, or service station. In addition,

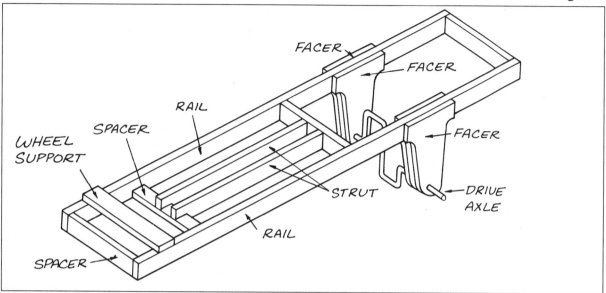

1 square = 1 inch

Figure C

Figure D

5. Align the two Rails and insert one end of the bent drive axle into the rear hole in each piece. Use glue and screws to attach one of the Spacers between the rails, flush with the back ends as shown in **Figure B**. Install another Spacer between the Rails flush with the front ends. Install another Spacer flush with the bottom edge of the Rails 8¾ inches from the front end. Install the last Spacer 31¼ inches from the front end.

6. A Wheel Support attached on top of the frame supports the axle assembly. Cut the 2 x 11½-inch Support from ¾-inch plywood. Drill a ⁵⁄₁₆-inch-diameter hole through the Support, 5¾ inches from one end, centered between the long edges. Install the Wheel Support on top of the frame Rails, 3¾ inches from the front end (**Figure B**).

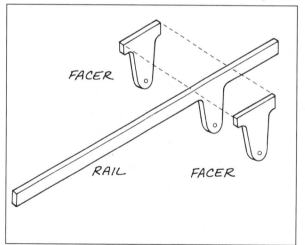

Figure E

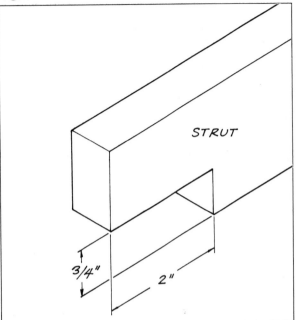

STRUT

3/4"

2"

7. Two Struts are attached to the frame to support the pedal assembly. Cut two 2 x 22½-inch Struts from ¾-inch plywood. Cut a ¾ x 2-inch notch in one end of each Strut, as shown in **Figure E**. Center the Struts between the Rails, and attach them between the two middle spacers, placing the notch over the forward one as shown in **Figure B**. Allow 1½ inches between the Struts, as shown. Temporarily secure both ends of each Strut with small holding nails.

Rear Axle and Pedal Assembly

A diagram of the assembled pedal mechanism is provided in **Figure F**.

1. The bent drive axle is already in place. When the pedals are pushed, this axle rotates to turn the rear wheels. For this reason, the wheels on the drive axle must be secured tightly so they will spin as the axle does. Perform the following procedures at each end of the drive axle. First, insert a cotter pin through the hole that was drilled 2 inches from the end. Add a flat

Figure F

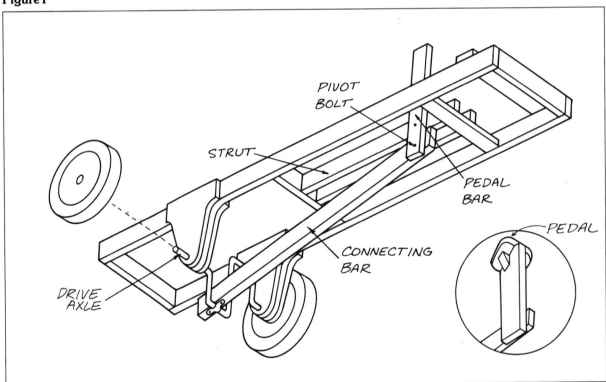

PIVOT
BOLT

STRUT

PEDAL
BAR

CONNECTING
BAR

PEDAL

DRIVE
AXLE

washer, a wheel, another flat washer, and a lock washer. Install a hex nut and tighten it until the wheel is securely wedged against the inner washer and the cotter pin.

2. For the pedal mechanism, cut the following pieces from ¾-inch plywood: two Connecting Bars, each 2 x 24 inches; two Pedal Bars, each 2 x 14 inches; and two Pedals, each 3 x 4 inches. Round off the corners of each Pedal using sandpaper.

3. The Connecting Bars are attached to the drive axle at one end, and to the Pedal Bars at the opposite end. To install one Connecting Bar on the drive axle, attach one flange of a conduit clamp 1 inch from one end of the lower edge of the Bar (**Figure G**). Place the Bar over one throw of the axle and slip the clamp over the axle as shown. Install the remaining clamp flange to the Connecting Bar. Attach the other Connecting Bar to the opposite drive axle throw in the same manner.

4. A hole drilled through each Connecting Bar near the opposite end will accommodate the pivot bolt that joins the Connecting Bar to the Pedal Bar (**Figure F**). Drill a ⁵⁄₁₆-inch-diameter hole through each Connecting Bar, 1½ inches from the front end.

5. Drill two ⁵⁄₁₆-inch-diameter holes through each Pedal Bar: one 1½ inches from one end, and one 6 inches from the first hole, measuring center to center, as shown in **Figure H**.

6. Join a Pedal Bar to the outer side of each Connecting Bar in the following manner: First, slip a flat washer over the end of a bolt. Insert the bolt through the hole near the end of the Pedal Bar, then add another flat washer. Insert the bolt through the hole near the front end of the Connecting Bar, add another flat washer, and install the hex nut. Be sure to leave this assembly loose enough to rotate easily.

7. Rotate the drive axle until the back end of one Connecting Bar is at the very bottom of its rotation cycle. The other Connecting Bar will now be at the top of its cycle. Chock the wheels so the axle will not turn as you work. At the front end of the Connecting Bar that is at the bottom of its cycle, move the Pedal Bar to a vertical position. Place the Pedal Bar against the outer side of the frame Strut (**Figure F**), and adjust it

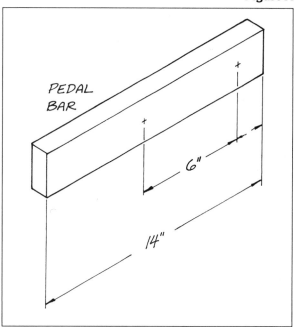

up or down until the center hole in the Pedal Bar is midway between the top and bottom edges of the Strut. (Make sure the Bar is still in a vertical position.) Mark the position of the hole on the Strut, remove the Strut from the frame, and drill a ⁵⁄₁₆-inch-diameter hole through the Strut at the mark. Replace the Strut, and secure with glue and screws. Slip a washer over the end

Figure I

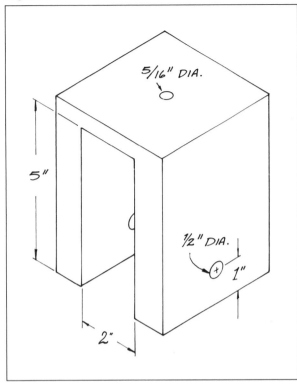

Figure J

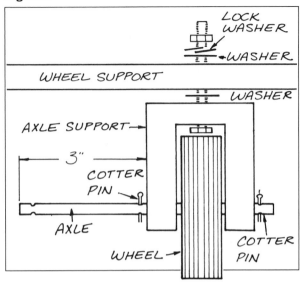

of a bolt and insert it through the Pedal Bar. Add another washer, insert the bolt through the Strut, add a third washer, and install the nut, leaving the assembly loose enough to pivot.

8. Rotate the drive axle one-half turn, so that the free Connecting Bar is at the bottom of its cycle, and repeat the procedures in step 7 to join the remaining Connecting Bar to the other Pedal Bar and Strut.

Note: It may be necessary to trim the tops of the Pedal Bars to make them a more comfortable length for your child. The Pedals, therefore, will be attached after you have built and attached the seat, and can adjust the length of the Pedal Bars to accommodate your sidewalk astronaut.

Front Axle and Steering Assembly

1. For the Axle Support, cut a 2 x 5-inch slot in the pine 4 x 4, as shown in **Figure I**. (We used a band saw to cut the slot.) For the axle, drill a ½-inch-diameter

hole through both extensions of the Support, 1 inch from the lower end, as shown. In addition, drill a ⁵⁄₁₆-inch-diameter hole down through the center of the top of the Support.

2. To install the Axle Support on the frame Wheel Support, insert a bolt up through the hole in the top of the Axle Support, add a washer, and push the bolt through the hole in the Wheel Support (**Figure J**). Add a washer, a lock washer, and install a hex nut on the end of the bolt. Tighten the nut, but not so much that it prevents the Axle Support from turning on the bolt.

3. Insert the axle through one hole in the Support, slip a wheel up into the notch in the Wheel Support, and push the axle through the wheel and the opposite side of the Support so that one end extends approximately 3 inches from the side, as shown in **Figure J**. To secure the wheel, insert a cotter pin through the axle hole on each side of the Support.

4. For the steering assembly, cut a Connecting Bar, 2 x 26½ inches from ¾-inch plywood. Drill a ⁵⁄₁₆-inch-diameter bolt hole through the Bar, ¾ inch from one end. Drill a 1-inch-diameter hole ¾ inch from the opposite end of the Bar, as shown in **Figure K**. In addition, drill a hole large enough to accommodate a 20d nail down through the Bar from edge to edge ¾ inch from the same end, as shown.

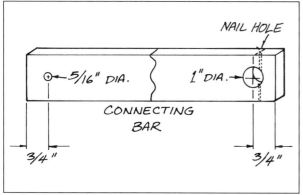

NAIL HOLE

5/16" DIA.   1" DIA.

CONNECTING
BAR

3/4"   3/4"

Figure L

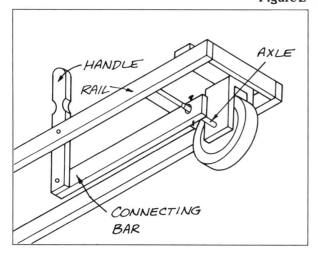

HANDLE
RAIL
AXLE
CONNECTING
BAR

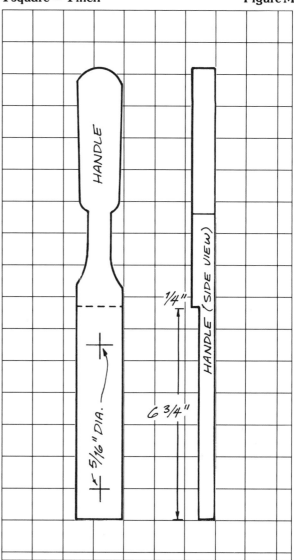

HANDLE

HANDLE (SIDE VIEW)

1/4"

5/16" DIA.   6 3/4"

5. Cut a Handle, 1½ x 14¼ inches, from ¾-inch plywood. A scale drawing for the Handle contours is provided in **Figure M**. Enlarge the drawing, transfer the pattern to the Handle, and cut the contours. One side of the Handle must be lap cut to provide steering control. Cut a ¼ x 6¾-inch lap along one lower side of the Handle, as shown in **Figure M**. Drill a 5/16-inch-diameter bolt hole through the Handle, 1 inch from the lower end. In addition, drill another bolt hole of the same size 4¼ inches above the first one.

6. The steering assembly is shown in **Figure L**. To begin, drill a 5/16-inch-diameter bolt hole through the right-hand frame Rail, 29½ inches from the front end. To attach the Handle to the Rail, place the lap cut against the inside of the Rail, as shown. Insert a bolt

through the hole, push it through the upper Handle hole, add a washer, lock washer, and install a hex nut, as shown. Attach the end of the Connecting Bar with the bolt hole to the lower end of the Handle in the same manner. To attach the Bar to the axle, slip the large hole over the extending end of the axle as shown and insert a 20d nail down through the nail hole. Tap the nail down through the axle hole and through the opposite nail hole in the Bar, as shown.

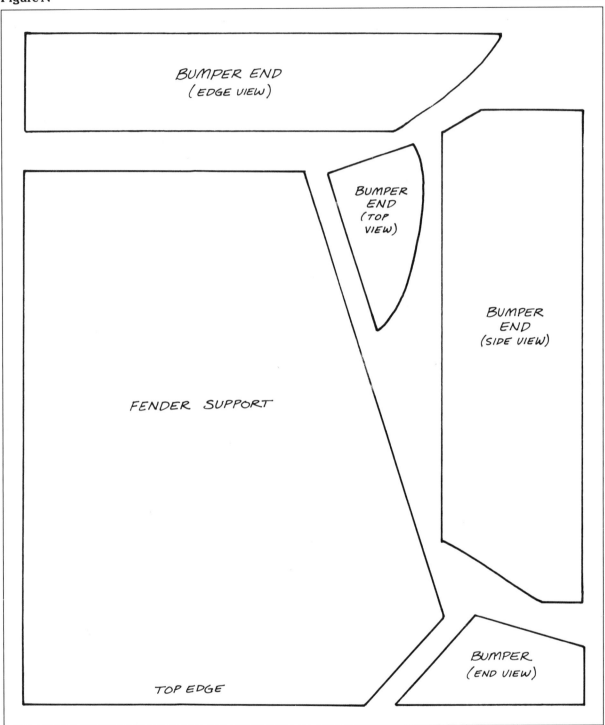

BUMPER END
(EDGE VIEW)

BUMPER
END
(TOP
VIEW)

BUMPER
END
(SIDE VIEW)

FENDER   SUPPORT

BUMPER
(END VIEW)

TOP EDGE

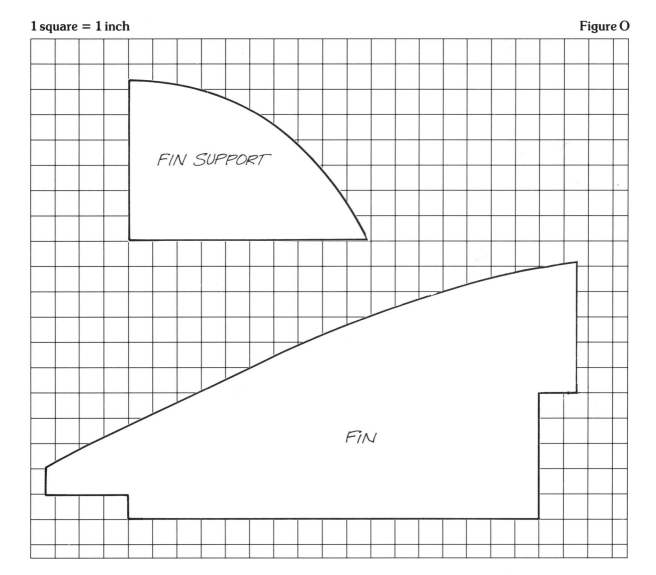

Building the Nose Cone

The nose cone consists of a Bumper, Fenders, Ribs, and Fins. The rib section is covered with an anti-alien canvas skin and a clear thermoplastic windshield.

1. Full-size patterns for the Bumper, Bumper Ends, and Fender Supports are provided in **Figure N**. **Figure P** illustrates the finished shape of the pieces. Refer to this illustration while you cut these pieces. For the Bumper, cut one 2 x 11⅝-inch piece from 2 x 4. Transfer the end view pattern and cut the bevels where

indicated. For the Bumper Ends, transfer the side view pattern and cut two Bumper Ends from 2 x 4. Cut contours on one Bumper End, using the end and edge views. Cut the remaining Bumper End so that the contours are a mirror image of the first piece. For the Fender Supports, transfer the pattern and cut two Fender Supports from ¾-inch plywood.

2. Scale drawings for the Fins and Fin Supports are provided in **Figure O**. Enlarge the drawings in **Figure O** to full size and cut two Fins and two Fin Supports from ¾-inch plywood.

Figure P

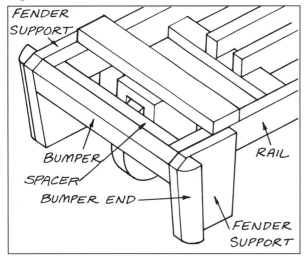

Figure Q

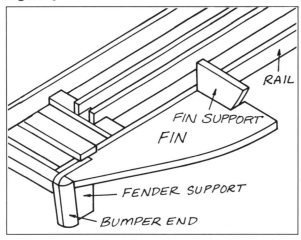

3. The assembled bumper is shown in **Figure P**. To begin, attach the Bumper to the front of the frame so that the 45-degree-beveled corner is even with the upper edge of the frame, as shown. Attach a Fender Support to the outside of one frame Rail aligning one corner with the beveled Bumper edge, and with the angled edge facing out, as shown. Attach the remaining Fender Support to the opposite side of the frame in the same manner. Attach a Bumper End to one Fender Support, aligning the front and top edges as shown. Attach the remaining Bumper End to the opposite Fender Support in the same manner.

4. To attach one Fin, butt the long straight edge against one frame Rail with the notch against the Fender Support and Bumper End, as shown in **Figure Q**. The Fin should be even with the upper edge of the frame. Attach the Fin using glue and screws inserted through the frame Rail into the Fin. To support the rear edge of the Fin, butt the straight edge of a Fin Support against the frame Rail with one side against the Fin notch, as shown. Attach the Fin Support to the frame Rail and the Fin using glue and screws. Attach the remaining Fin and Fin Support on the opposite side of the frame in the same manner.

5. Scale drawings for the A, B, C, and D Ribs are provided in **Figure R**. Enlarge the drawings and cut two of each Rib from ¾-inch plywood. To contour the D Rib, round off one long edge completely, as shown in the inset in **Figure R**.

6. The ribs are attached between the bumper and a Rim that forms the spaceship dashboard (**Figure T**). One portion of the Rim is cut out to fit over the frame Rails as shown. To save time later, we suggest that you cut the Rim and the front circle of the cargo bay simultaneously. For the two pieces, cut two 23½-inch-diameter circles from ¾-inch plywood. Nail the two circles together temporarily while you cut a notch. To cut the notch, mark two points on the outer edge of one circle, 11½ inches apart, and draw a straight line between the points (**Figure S**). Use a carpenter's square to draw a 3-inch line at a 90-degree angle up from each end of the longer line, as shown. Draw a straight line connecting the ends of the short lines as shown. Cut out the notch along the lines using a sabre saw. Disassemble the circles, and cut a 17½-inch-diameter circle in the center of one circle to make the Rim (**Figure S**).

7. One side of the assembled rib section is shown in **Figure T**. To begin, slip the Rim notch over the frame Rails and place the Rim against the Fin Supports so that the lower edges are aligned. Attach the Rim to the Fin Supports using glue and screws. Attach one end of an A Rib to one frame Rail directly behind the Bumper as shown. Attach the upper end of the A Rib to the Rim as shown. The B and C Ribs are attached between the Fin and A Rib, as shown. With the upper end against the A Rib, position the lower end of a B Rib 2¾ inches from the Fin Support. Attach the upper end of the B Rib

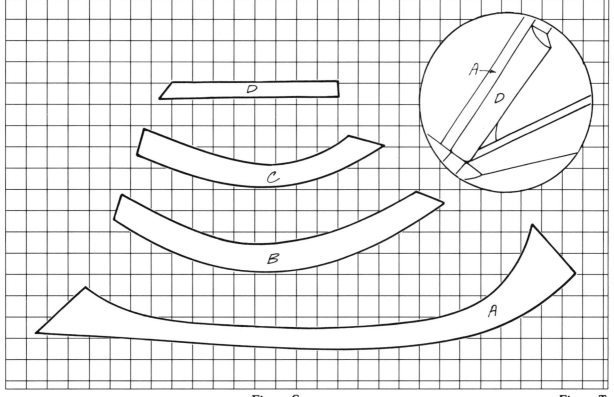

Figure S

Figure T

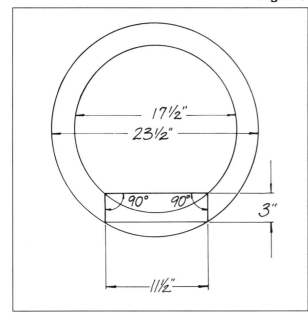

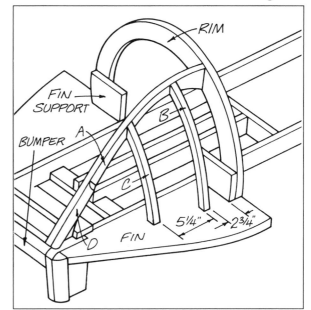

Figure U   1 square = 1 inch

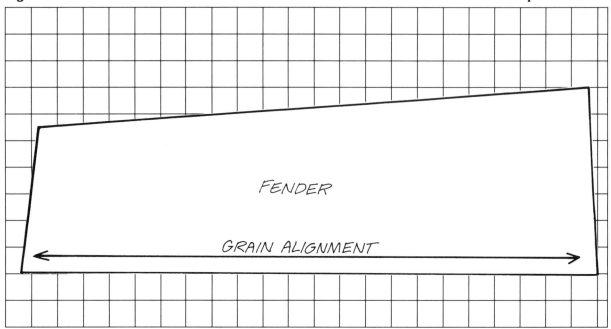

FENDER

GRAIN ALIGNMENT

Figure V

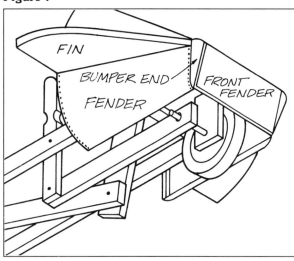

FIN

BUMPER END
FENDER

FRONT
FENDER

to the **A** Rib, and the lower end to the Fin using glue and screws. Position and attach a **C** Rib 5¼ inches from the **B** Rib as shown. Attach a **D** Rib along the outer side of the **A** Rib, aligning the curved edges of both pieces, as shown. Attach the remaining **A**, **B**, **C**, and **D** Ribs on the opposite side of the nose cone in the same manner.

8. A scale drawing for the Fender is provided in **Figure U**. Enlarge the drawing and cut two Fenders from ⅛-inch plywood. The Fenders will have to bend without splitting, so when you cut them, be sure that the wood grain is aligned with the long straight edge. In addition, cut one Front Fender from ⅛-inch plywood, 5 x 13¼ inches.

9. To install one Fender, place the longer edge against the underside of a Fin, with the shorter end overlapping the Bumper End, as shown in **Figure V**. Carefully nail the front end along the curved edge of the Bumper End as shown. Nail the rear end along the curved edge of the Fin Support and Rim, carefully bending the Fender as you go. Install the remaining Fender on the opposite side of the spaceship in the same manner. To install the Front Fender, nail it over the front edges of the Fender Supports with one long edge along the beveled Bumper edge as shown.

10. The canvas skin is stretched over the rib assembly on the sides of the nose cone and cut after it is in place. To begin, cut two 23-inch lengths of pine lattice and nail one along the bottom of the rib assembly on each side of the nose cone, as shown in **Figure W**. To

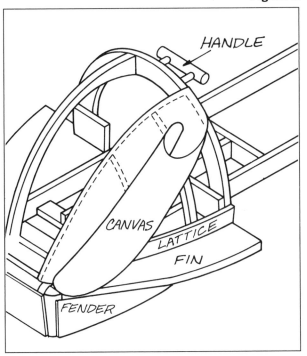

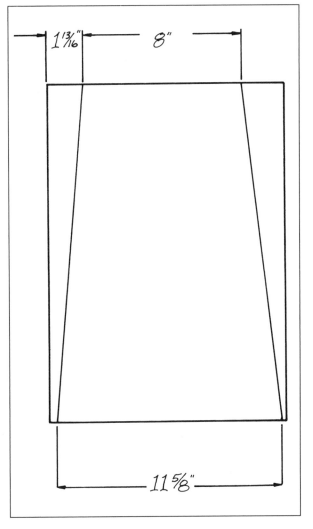

install the canvas skin on one side, run a bead of silicone caulk or hot melt glue along the upper edge of the **A** Rib and allow it to set until tacky. Press one end of the canvas along the glued edge of the rib as shown. Apply glue to the upper curved edge of the **B** and **C** Ribs and the Rim, and stretch the canvas down over them, as shown. Apply glue to the side of the lattice and press the canvas in place along it. Cut the canvas along the lower lattice edge using a razor blade knife. Repeat the procedure on the opposite side of the nose cone, using the remaining canvas. To secure the canvas further, insert decorative upholstery tacks along the Rim edge on each side.

11. For the handle, cut a 7-inch length of 1¼-inch-diameter dowel rod and two 1-inch lengths of ¾-inch-diameter dowel rod. Drill a ¾-inch-diameter socket ¾ inch from each end of the larger-diameter dowel and insert a short dowel piece in each socket. Insert and countersink a screw from the opposite side of the large dowel into the end of each short piece. To install the assembled handle on the Rim, insert a screw through the Rim into each short dowel, as shown in **Figure W**.

12. A cutting diagram for the Windshield is provided in **Figure X**. Cut one Windshield from the thermoplastic. Wait to install the Windshield until you've painted the spaceship.

Building the Seat and Tail Section

The seat is attached to the frame rails and can be positioned to accommodate your child's size. The tail section consists of a drum-shaped cargo bay that you can adjust to fit behind the seat. It features nine main rockets and four external thrusters mounted on fins.

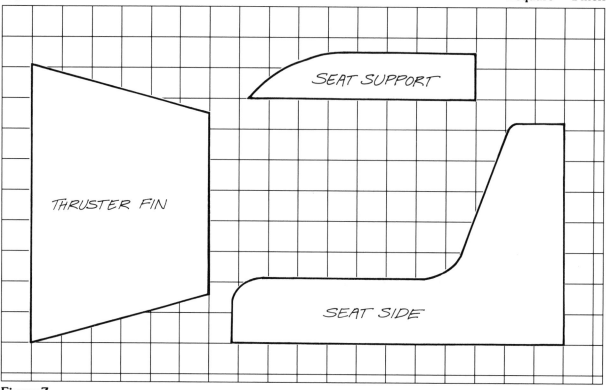

THRUSTER FIN

SEAT SUPPORT

SEAT SIDE

Figure Z

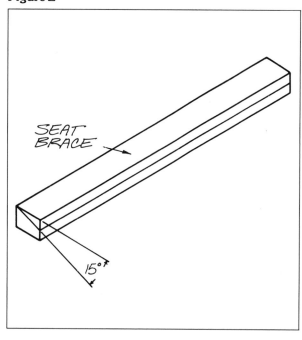

SEAT BRACE

15°

1. Scale drawings for the Seat Side and Seat Support are provided in **Figure Y**. Enlarge the drawings and cut two Seat Sides from ½-inch plywood. Cut two Seat Supports from ¾-inch plywood. Cut one 11½ x 1-inch Seat Brace from ¾-inch plywood. Bevel one long edge at a 15-degree angle, as shown in **Figure Z**. In addition, cut two 6¾ x 11½-inch Seat Back/Floors from ¾-inch plywood. Round off one long edge of each Back/Floor.

2. To install the seat, temporarily attach the Seat Brace across the frame Rails, 21¼ inches from the rear end of the frame, so that the beveled edge is on top, as shown in **Figure AA**. Temporarily attach the Seat Floor to the Brace, placing the rounded edge toward the front as shown. Have your child sit on the Seat Floor and place his feet on the ends of the Pedal Bars to check the position of the seat. Adjust it farther from or closer to the front of the spaceship to get a good fit, and permanently attach the Seat Brace and Seat Floor to the frame using glue and screws. Install one Seat

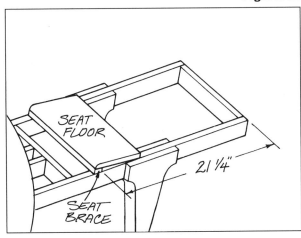

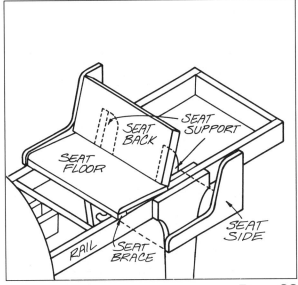

Support on the inner side of each frame Rail positioned so that the front edge is at a 15-degree angle, as shown in **Figure BB**. Attach one end of the Seat Back to each Support, butting the Back-to-Floor edge as shown. Attach a Seat Side to each end of the Seat Back and Floor, aligning the lower edge of the Seat Side with the upper edge of the frame Rail, as shown.

3. The cargo bay consists of the notched front circle you cut earlier, and a 23½-inch-diameter rear circle, cut from ¾-inch plywood. Drill nine 1¾-inch-diameter holes through the unnotched circle to accommodate the PVC rockets, as shown in **Figure CC**.

4. Cut an 11½ x 60-inch piece of ⅛-inch plywood to cover the cargo bay. Note: If you re-positioned the seat farther toward the rear of the spaceship, measure the distance between the rear edge of the Seat Supports and the end of the frame, and add ¾-inch to determine the width of the cargo bay cover. A scale drawing for the Thruster Fin is provided in **Figure Y**. Enlarge the drawing to make a full-size paper pattern. Transfer the pattern and cut four Fins from ¾-inch plywood. In addition, cut four 15-inch lengths of 1¼-inch-diameter dowel to serve as the Thruster Rockets. Cut four 1¼ x 8-inch Fin Supports from ¾-inch plywood.

5. The assembled cargo bay is shown in **Figure DD**. To begin, place the notched front circle on top of the drilled rear circle and trace along the notched edge with a pencil. Attach the notched circle 10½ inches from the rear end of the frame using glue and screws as shown.

Figure CC

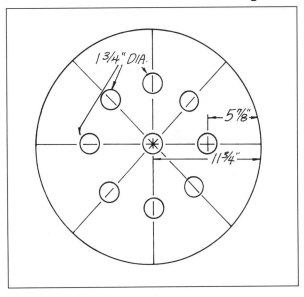

(If you re-positioned the seat, attach the circle immediately behind the Seat Supports.) The drilled circle must be aligned with the notched circle when it is attached to the frame. To align the circles, place the drilled circle against the frame so that the outline of the notch is even with the upper edge of the frame. Attach the circle to the frame using glue and screws.

Figure DD

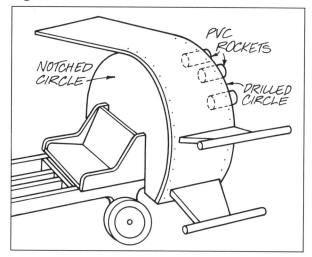

Figure EE

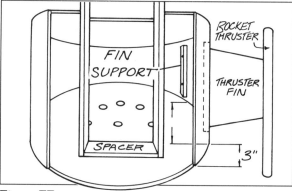

Figure FF

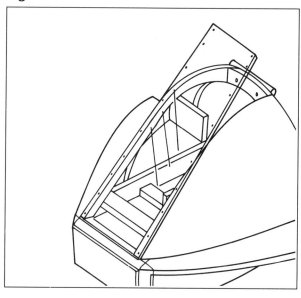

6. To attach the plywood along the curved edges of the cargo bay, place one end at the lower edge of the notched circle. Nail the plywood along the edge of each circle, bending it as you go, until you reach the opposite lower edge.

7. Install one Fin Support inside the cargo bay between the front and rear circles, 3 inches from the lower edge of the plywood cover. A view from the underside is shown in **Figure EE**. Install another Fin Support 8½ inches above the first one. Install the remaining Fin Supports on the opposite side of the cargo bay.

8. Install one Thruster Fin on the outside of the cargo bay aligned with the Fin Support on the inside, (**Figure EE**). Insert two screws from inside the cargo bay through the Fin Support into the Fin. Install the remaining Thruster Fins in the same manner. Attach one Rocket Thruster to the end of each Thruster Fin.

9. The main rockets are cut from PVC pipe and glued into the holes in the back of the cargo bay. For the rockets, cut nine 3-inch lengths of PVC pipe. Insert one Rocket into each cargo bay hole and glue in place.

Final Countdown

1. Paint the spaceship.

2. To attach the windshield, drill nine screw holes along each long side. To make the plastic more pliable, heat it slightly — outdoors in the sun on a hot day, or under a heat lamp. Position the windshield over the opening in the nose cone, as shown in **Figure FF**. Begin at the lower wide end and insert a screw through each hole into the edge of the nose cone ribs, as shown. As you work your way up the windshield, bend the plastic very carefully so it won't crack. At the very top, we suggest that you heat the plastic using a hair drier to avoid cracking it.

3. Before you prepare for takeoff, have your astronaut sit in the seat and test the length of the Pedal Bars. Cut off the top of the Pedal Bars if necessary to make them a more comfortable length. Trim the back upper corner of each Bar to accommodate the Pedal. Glue a Pedal to each Bar and secure with screws.

Tractor

We modeled this riding machine after a familiar sight here in Oklahoma farm country – where the corn grows as high as an elephant's eye! It's a pedal-powered tractor, sure to mow down the sidewalk competition and plow new ground in toddler locomotion. Overall dimensions: 25 x 32 x 51 inches.

Figure A

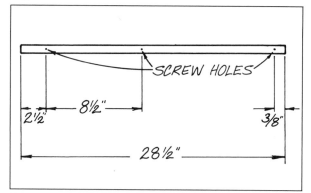

Figure B

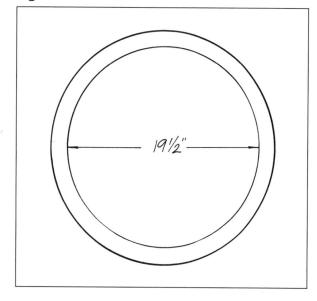

Materials

17 x 50-inch piece of ⅛-inch exterior-grade plywood.

23 x 27-inch piece of ¼-inch exterior-grade plywood.

34 x 48-inch piece of ½-inch exterior-grade plywood.

4 x 8-foot sheet of ¾-inch exterior-grade plywood.

1-foot length of pine 1 x 6.

1-inch length of pine 2 x 2.

20-inch length of pine 2 x 4.

2-foot length of ¼-inch-diameter wooden dowel rod.

2-foot length of ½-inch-diameter wooden dowel rod.

16-inch length of wooden closet rod, 1½ inches in diameter.

3-foot length of 4-inch-diameter PVC pipe. (Note: PVC pipe is sized by internal diameter.)

One 1½-inch-diameter spherical wooden drawer pull.

Four ½-inch-diameter metal rods in the following lengths: one 6¼ inches, one 18½ inches, one 25½ inches, and one 28½ inches. The 18½-inch rod will serve as the front axle, and must be drilled ⅜ inch from each end to accommodate a cotter pin. The 25½-inch rod will serve as the rear axle, and must be drilled ⅜ inch from each end to accommodate a No. 6 gauge set screw. The longest rod will serve as the steering column. It must be drilled 2½ and 10½ inches from one end, and ⅜ inch from the opposite end (**Figure A**), to accommodate No. 6 gauge set screws. The shortest rod must be drilled 1⅛ inches from each end, to accommodate an 8d nail. All of the holes in each rod should be drilled along the same axis. If your drill is not designed for this job, ask for help at a hardware shop, machine shop, or service station.

Ten 1½-inch-diameter flat washers that will fit on the ½-inch-diameter axle rods.

Two metal pulleys, each one having a ½-inch-diameter bore: one 4 inches in diameter, and one 4½ inches in diameter.

One 48-inch V-belt, ½ inch wide.

6-foot length of ⅛-inch-diameter plastic-covered cable.

Two cotter pins.

One 3½-inch-long carriage bolt, ½-inch in diameter with two flat washers, a lock washer, and hex nut to fit.

Four ¾-inch-diameter plastic washers. You can cut these from an old plastic bottle.

Six eyescrews, each ½ inch in diameter.

8d common nails, 4d finishing nails, and 1-inch-long escutcheon nails.

Two sheet metal screws, each 1 inch long.

A large handful of No. 6 gauge flathead wood screws, 1¼ inches long; two No. 6 gauge roundhead wood screws, each ¾ inch long; and two ½-inch-diameter flat metal washers to fit the ¾-inch screws.

Waterproof glue.

Exterior paint in your choice of colors. We used green, yellow, and black.

Cutting the Pieces

There are lots and lots of parts to cut, so label each one with its identifying code letter and/or its name. This will prevent confusion later on, when you're deep in the throes of assembly.

1. Cut the pieces listed here from ¾-inch plywood. Label each piece with its identifying code letter.

Code	Dimensions	Quantity
A	23½-inch-diameter circle	6
B	11½-inch-diameter circle	4
C	3½ x 43¼ inches	2
D	3½ x 20 inches	2
E	3½ x 15½ inches	3
F	3 x 15½ inches	1
G	2¼ x 15½ inches	2
H	2¼ x 10½ inches	1
I	3½ x 15 inches	1
J	3½ x 13½ inches	2
K	2¼ x 23 inches	2
L	2¼ x 12 inches	2
M	11 x 20 inches	2

2. Four of the A Wheels must be cut to create wheel rims. Cut a 19½-inch-diameter circle from the center of each of four A Wheels, as shown in **Figure B**. Label each Wheel Rim A. From the remaining pieces that were cut from the centers, cut and label the pieces listed here.

Code	Dimensions	Quantity
N	3 x 3½ inches	2
O	3½ x 5½ inches	2
P	3 x 5 inches	1
Q	3 x 3½ inches	1
R	3½ x 5 inches	2
S	2½-inch-diameter circle	4
T	8-inch-diameter circle	1

3. Two of the B Wheels must be cut to create wheel rims and pedal sprockets. Carefully cut an 8½-inch-diameter circle from the center of each of two B Wheels. Label the Wheel Rims B. Label the center circles as U

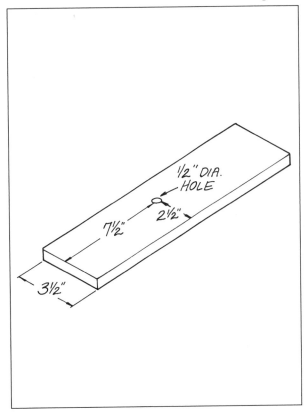

Figure C

Pedal Sprockets. Drill a ½-inch-diameter hole 1½ inches from the curved outer edge of each U Sprocket to accommodate the pedal shaft. In addition, drill a ½-inch-diameter axle hole through the exact center of each U Sprocket.

4. The E pieces will support the pedal sprocket axle. Temporarily nail together the two E pieces, and drill a ½-inch-diameter hole through both, 7½ inches from one end and 2½ inches from one long edge, as shown in **Figure C**. Remove the holding nails.

5. The F and P pieces will support the upper end of the steering column. Drill a ½-inch-diameter hole through the P piece at a 40-degree angle, centered between the long edges and ⅝ inch from one end, as shown in **Figure D**. Drill a hole of the same size and at the same angle through the F piece, centered between the long edges and 4¾ inches from one end as shown in **Figure D**.

Figure D

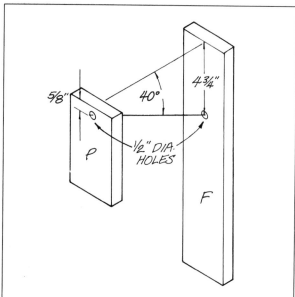

6. A scale drawing for the **M** Seat is provided in **Figure E**. Enlarge the drawing and cut one Seat from each of the rectangular **M** pieces that you cut in step 1. Both Seat pieces must be grooved to accommodate the V-belt that connects the pedals to the rear axle. In one **M** Seat, cut a 1⅛ x 2-inch groove where indicated on the scale drawing. Cut a 2 x 15¼-inch groove into the remaining Seat where indicated. A scale drawing for the Seat Support is provided in **Figure E**. Enlarge the drawing to full size and cut one Seat Support from ⅛-inch plywood.

7. The **Q** piece will house the pivot bolt that supports the front axle assembly, and must be drilled as shown in **Figure F**. Drill a ½-inch-diameter hole through the center of the **Q** piece to accommodate the pivot bolt. In addition, the **Q** piece will support the lower end of the steering column. Drill a ½-inch-diameter socket at a 40-degree angle, centered between the bolt hole and one short end, as shown.

Figure E

1 square = 1 inch

FENDER SUPPORT

PLACEMENT LINE →

SEAT SUPPORT

MIDDLE OF BACK

SEAT

CUT TO HERE FOR BOTTOM SEAT

CUT TO HERE FOR TOP SEAT

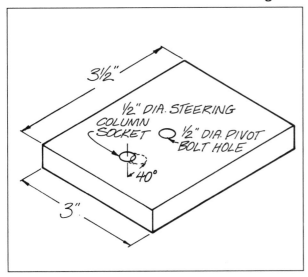

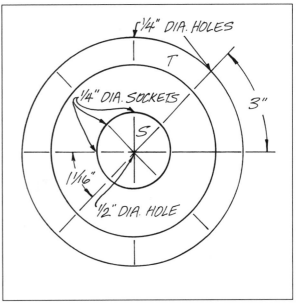

8. The steering wheel will consist of a rim, a double hub, and eight spokes. To create the rim, cut a 5½-inch-diameter circle from the center of the T piece. Label the rim T Steering Rim. To accommodate the spokes, drill eight ¼-inch-diameter holes through the Rim, from the outer edge to the inner edge, spaced at 3-inch intervals as shown in **Figure G**. The double hub will consist of two **S** pieces. Drill eight ¼-inch-diameter sockets into the edge of one S Hub, each ½ inch deep and spaced at 1¹⁄₁₆-inch intervals, as shown in **Figure G**. These sockets will accommodate the spokes. Glue a second S Hub to the drilled Hub, and drill a ½-inch-diameter hole through the exact center of both. Label this assembly as the Steering Wheel Hub. The layer with the sockets will be the bottom layer. Drill a ⅛-inch-diameter set screw hole into the upper layer, from the outer edge to the center hole. For the Steering Wheel Spokes, cut eight 3-inch lengths of ¼-inch-diameter dowel rod, and label them as such.

9. Cut the pieces listed here from ¼-inch plywood.

Code	Dimensions	Quantity
V	17 x 20 inches	1
W	17 x 29 inches	1
X	13½ x 24 inches	2
Y	12 x 15½ inches	2

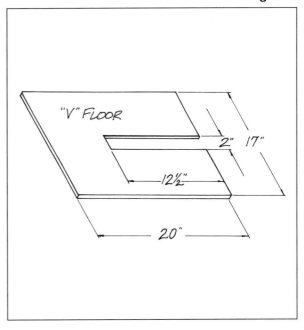

10. The V piece will serve as the upper floor of the tractor frame, and must be grooved to accommodate the V-belt. Cut a 2 x 12½-inch groove into the center of one end, as shown in **Figure H**.

Figure I

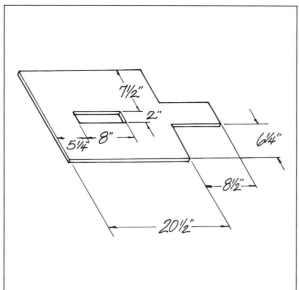

Figure K

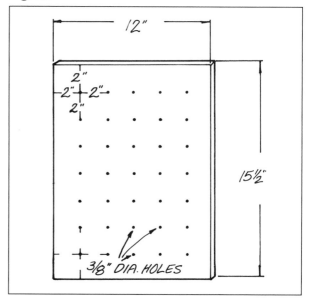

Figure J

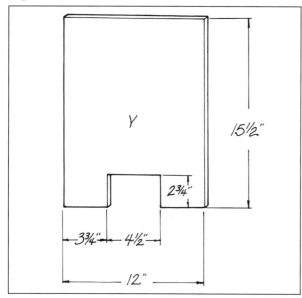

11. The **W** piece will serve as the lower floor of the tractor frame. A cutting diagram for the **W** Floor is provided in **Figure I**. Cut a 6¼ x 8½-inch rectangle from each of two adjacent corners at one end, as shown. To accommodate the rear axle pulley and V-belt, cut a 2 x 8-inch slot, 5¼ inches from the opposite end.

12. The **Y** pieces will serve as the front and back of the radiator. Cut a 2¾ x 4½-inch notch at one end of one **Y** Radiator, as shown in **Figure J**. The remaining **Y** Radiator is drilled to create the illusion of an air-intake plate, as shown in **Figure K**, but these holes are purely decorative so placement is not crucial. We drilled thirty-five ⅜-inch-diameter holes through the **Y** piece, spaced 2 inches apart in seven horizontal rows, with 2 inches between rows. The first row should be 2 inches from one end as shown.

13. A scale drawing for the Fender Support is provided in **Figure E**. Enlarge the drawing and cut two Fender Supports from ½-inch plywood. Be sure to transfer the placement lines from the pattern to the wood. In addition, cut two 4 x 35-inch Fenders from ⅛-inch plywood.

14. From 2 x 4, cut four 3¼-inch-diameter circles to serve as Rear Wheel Hubs. Drill a ½-inch-diameter hole through the center of each Hub. Two of these Hubs must also be drilled to accommodate a set screw. Drill a ⅛-inch-diameter hole from the curved outer edge to the center of each of two Hubs.

15. Cut a 3½-inch length of 2 x 4. To create two triangular glue blocks, cut the piece in half along the diagonal, cutting from corner to corner.

Figure L　　　　　　　　**Figure M**

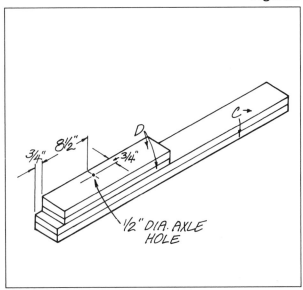

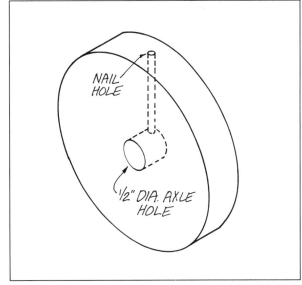

16. The R pieces will serve as part of the front axle support. Drill a ½-inch-diameter hole through each R piece, centered between the long edges and 1 inch from one end. For the rear axle support, temporarily nail together all of the C and D pieces as shown in **Figure L**, so that the C pieces extend ¾ inch beyond the D pieces at one end. Drill a ½-inch-diameter hole through the stack of C and D pieces where indicated in **Figure L**, ¾ inch from one long edge and 8½ inches from one end of the D pieces, as shown. When you have drilled the hole, remove the temporary holding nails and separate the pieces.

17. Cut two 3½-inch-diameter circular Sprocket Spacers from 1 x 6. Drill a ½-inch-diameter axle hole through the center of each Spacer. In addition, drill a hole large enough to accommodate an 8d nail, from the curved outer edge to the center of each Spacer, as shown in **Figure M**.

18. Each pedal consists of Pins and a Shaft mounted between two Frame pieces. Cut four 2¾-inch-long Pedal Pins and two 3¾-inch-long Pedal Shafts from ½-inch-diameter dowel rod. For the Pedal Frames, rip a ¼ x ¾ x 12-inch strip from 1 x 6. From the strip, cut four 2⅝-inch-long Pedal Frames. The Frames must be drilled to accommodate the Pedal Pins and Pedal

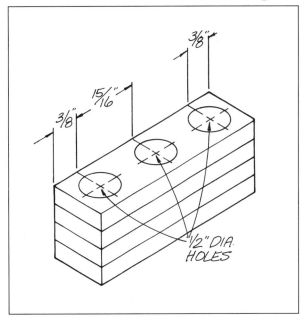

Shaft. Temporarily nail together the four Frames, and drill a ½-inch-diameter hole through the stack, ⅜ inch from each end, as shown in **Figure N**. In addition, drill another ½-inch-diameter hole centered between the end holes, as shown. Remove the holding nails.

Figure O

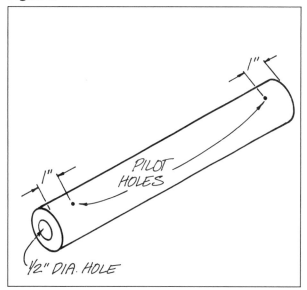

Figure P

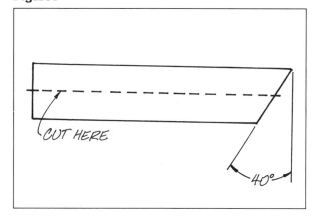

19. Cut a 10-inch length of 1½-inch-diameter closet rod to serve as the steering column Cable Clamp. Drill a screw hole through the Cable Clamp, 1 inch from each end, as shown in **Figure O**. In addition, drill a ½-inch-diameter hole through the center length of the Cable Clamp, as shown. Cut a 4½-inch length of 1½-inch-diameter closet rod to serve as the Steering Column Spacer. Drill a ½-inch-diameter hole through the center length of the Spacer in the same manner as you did for the Cable Clamp. In addition, miter one end of the Spacer at a 40-degree angle, and then cut the Spacer in half lengthwise as shown in **Figure P**.

Assembling the Frame and Front Axle Support

1. The assembled tractor frame is shown in **Figure Q**. The pieces should be assembled with the ends and edges butted together exactly as shown. Use glue and either nails or screws for all joints. Begin by assembling the center rail section. Glue an O piece to one side of a C Rail, 18½ inches from the drilled end of the C Rail. Next, glue two N pieces to the same C Rail, one at each end as shown, with upper and lower edges flush. Attach the remaining O piece to the second C Rail just as you did for the first one, but be sure that it is placed on the proper side of the C piece. When the Rails are connected together as shown in **Figure Q**, the axle hole near the rear end of each Rail should be closer to the lower edge than to the upper edge. Glue this assembly to the N pieces that are attached to the first Rail.

2. To build the rear box section of the frame, attach the two D pieces and one E piece to the assembly you created in step 1, butting the ends as shown in **Figure Q**. Turn the D pieces so that the axle hole in each one is aligned with the axle holes in the C Rails. Use the glue blocks that you cut previously to strengthen the C-to-O joints as shown. Install the Q piece between the Rails, ¾ inch from the undrilled (front) ends of the Rails and flush with the lower edges. The Q piece should be turned so that the steering column socket is on the top, facing the back of the frame.

3. To install the 25½-inch rear axle, slide it through the hole in one D piece and on through one C Rail, as shown in **Figure Q**. Slip the 4½-inch-diameter pulley and the V-belt over the axle end, and then push the axle through the holes in the C Rail and D piece on the other side of the frame, as shown.

4. Install the W Lower Floor on the bottom of the rear box section of the frame. Be sure that the pulley is centered in the floor slot. The edges of the Floor should be flush with the sides of the box section.

5. Install one Fender Support against the outer side of one D piece, as shown in **Figure R**. The lower edge of the the Support should be ¾ inch below the upper edge of the D piece, and the placement line on the Support should match the upper rear corner of the box section. Insert screws through the Support into the D

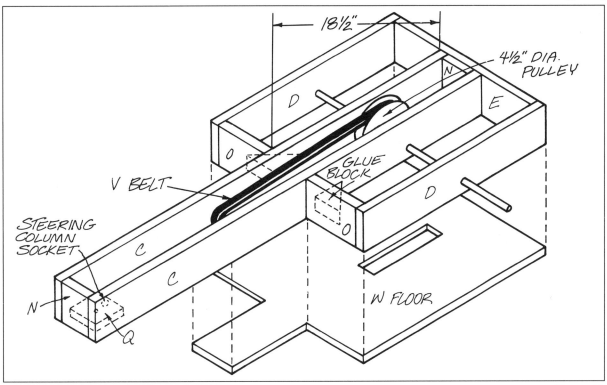

18½"

4½" DIA. PULLEY

D

N

E

O

V BELT

GLUE BLOCK

D

O

STEERING COLUMN SOCKET

C

C

N

Q

W FLOOR

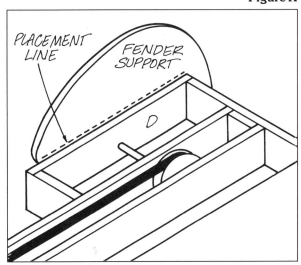

PLACEMENT LINE

FENDER SUPPORT

D

piece. Install the remaining Fender Support on the opposite side of the box section in the same manner.

6. The assembled front axle support is shown in **Figure S**. To begin, attach the R pieces to the I piece, butting the edges as shown. Be sure that the drilled end of each R piece is at the bottom. Position one J piece against the I piece as shown and attach it to the R piece at each end. Attach the remaining J piece between the R pieces, 1½ inches from the drilled ends, as shown. Drill a ½-inch-diameter pivot bolt hole down through center of the I and upper J pieces, as shown. The bolt hole should be centered between the long edges and between the ends.

7. To attach the front axle support to the frame, first place the assembled support underneath the front end of the frame. Align the bolt hole that you just drilled through the axle support with the bolt hole in the frame Q piece. Insert the carriage bolt down through the Q piece, add a flat washer, and then insert it through the axle support. Add a second flat washer, then the lock washer, and then the nut. This assembly should be left loose enough so that the axle support can swivel easily on the bolt.

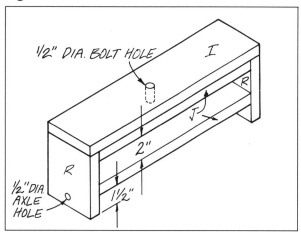

½" DIA. BOLT HOLE

I

R

J

2"

R

½" DIA.
AXLE
HOLE

1½"

Figure T

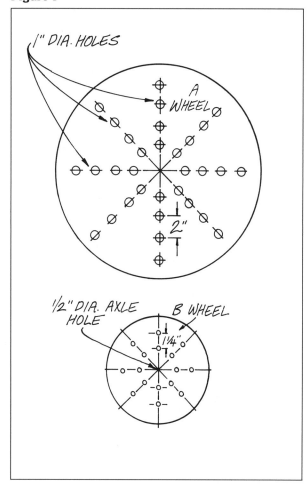

1" DIA. HOLES

A
WHEEL

2"

½" DIA. AXLE
HOLE

B WHEEL

1¼"

Assembling the Wheels

1. Each assembled wheel consists of a solid wheel piece, one or two rims, and one or two hubs. The solid wheel pieces are drilled to look like tractor wheels. To save time, we suggest that you temporarily nail together the two solid A Wheels and drill the holes through both simultaneously, then do the same with the two solid B Wheels. Drilling diagrams for both the large A and small B Wheels are provided in **Figure T**. The center hole indicated in each diagram will serve as the axle hole. Each of these holes should be ½ inch in diameter, and carefully placed in the exact center of the wheel. The rest of the holes are purely decorative, so exact placement is not important. We used a 1-inch-diameter drill bit for the decorative holes. Remove the holding nails when you have finished drilling the holes.

2. Each front wheel consists of one solid B Wheel, one B Rim, and one S Hub. (Use the two remaining single S pieces that were not used for the Steering Wheel Hub.) An assembled front wheel is shown in **Figure U**. To begin, glue one B Rim to one B Wheel, and secure by inserting screws through the Wheel into the Rim. Drill a ½-inch-diameter axle hole through the center of one S Hub. Attach the Hub to the center of the partially assembled Wheel, on the same side as the Rim, using glue and four screws. Be sure to align the center axle holes of the Wheel and Hub. Assemble a second front wheel in the same manner.

3. Each rear wheel consists of one solid A Wheel, sandwiched between two A Rims and two Rear Wheel Hubs. An assembled rear wheel is shown in **Figure V**. To begin, glue one A Rim to one A Wheel, and secure by inserting screws through the Wheel into the Rim. Attach another A Rim to the opposite side of the Wheel, this time inserting the screws through the Rim into the Wheel. Choose one Rear Wheel Hub with a set screw hole, and one without. Glue the Hub with the set screw hole to the center of the Wheel on one side, aligning the center axle holes. Secure with four screws, being careful to avoid the set screw hole. Attach the second Hub on the opposite side of the Wheel in the same manner. Assemble a second rear wheel in the same manner as the first.

4. To install the front wheels, insert the 18½-inch front axle through the holes in the front axle support,

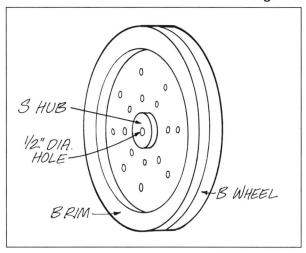

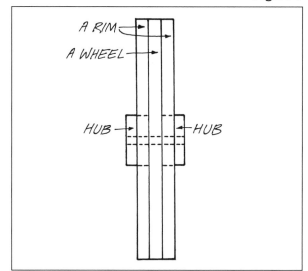

leaving equal extensions on each side. Slip a flat washer over one end of the axle, and then add a small front wheel (rim side out) and another flat washer. Insert a cotter pin through the hole near the end of the axle. Install the remaining front wheel on the other end of the axle in the same manner.

5. To install one rear wheel, slip two flat washers over one end of the rear axle. Install a large rear wheel, so that the hub with the set screw hole is on the outside. Turn the wheel a few times to be sure it does not bind on the Fender Support. Rotate the wheels on the axle until the set screw hole in the hub is aligned with the hole near the end of the axle, and then insert a screw into the set screw hole. Tighten the set screw to secure the wheel. Install the remaining rear wheel on the other end of the axle in the same manner.

Assembling the Pedal Mechanism

1. The pedal sprockets are anchored to a post that also supports the steering column and one end of the hood assembly. The assembled post is shown in **Figure W**. To begin, assemble the E and F pieces, butting the edges as shown. Be sure the holes in the E pieces are aligned and positioned farthest from the F piece, as shown. In addition, be sure the steering column hole in the F piece is above the axle holes in the E pieces. Attach the P piece so that the steering column hole is at the top, as shown.

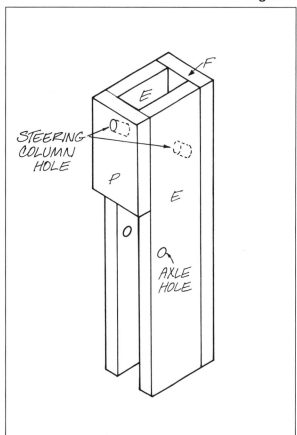

Figure X

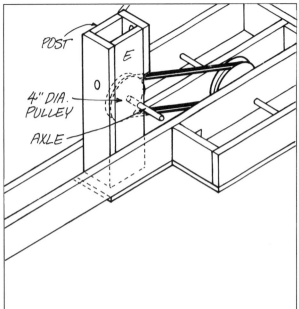

Figure Z

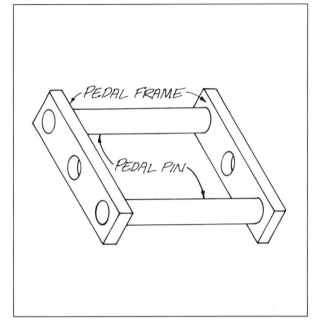

Figure Y

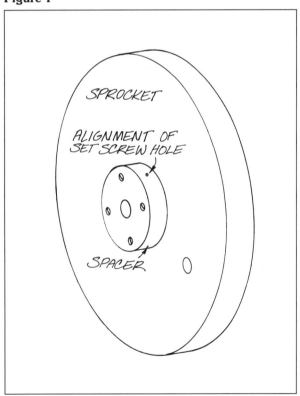

2. To install the assembled post, insert the lower end down between the frame rails so that it rests on the lower floor of the frame, as shown in **Figure X**. To install the 6¼-inch sprocket axle through the post, slip one end into the hole in one **E** piece. Inside the post, slip the 4-inch-diameter pulley over the end of the axle. Pull up the V-belt from the rear axle pulley, and loop the belt over the sprocket pulley. Push the axle on through the hole in the opposite **E** piece, leaving equal extensions on each side.

3. An assistant will be helpful for this step. Slide the post toward the front of the frame until the V-belt is tight. To place more tension on the belt, hold the upper end of the post in the same position, and slide the lower end another inch toward the front of the frame. Secure it with temporary holding nails. Drill a hole through the rail and post on each side of the frame, insert a screw into each of these holes, and remove the holding nails. Now pull the upper end of the post toward the front of the frame until it is vertical, as shown. Again, nail it in place temporarily while you drill a hole and insert a screw through the rail and post on each side of the frame. Remove the nails, and tighten the set screw on each pulley.

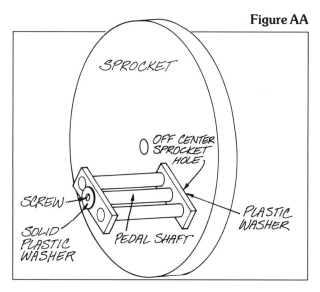

Figure AA

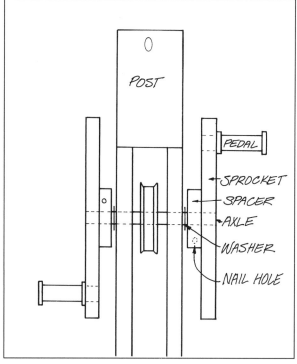

Figure BB

4. To assemble each pedal sprocket, you will be attaching a Sprocket Spacer to the center of a U Sprocket using glue and screws, as shown in **Figure Y**, but keep a couple of things in mind before you begin. Because a pedal will be attached to the off-center hole in each Sprocket, and because the pedals must be aligned at opposing edges of the Sprockets when you perform the final assembly later on, each Sprocket Spacer must be rotated correctly before it is attached to a Sprocket in this step. The proper rotation is shown in **Figure Y**. Place the two U Sprockets side by side on a flat surface, and rotate them until the off-center hole in each Sprocket is on the right-hand side as shown. Look at one Sprocket Spacer, and find the set screw hole that was drilled from the outer edge to the center hole. Place this Sprocket Spacer on top of one Sprocket, so that the set screw hole faces the top of the Sprocket, as shown in **Figure Y**. Be sure that the center holes are aligned, and permanently attach the Spacer to the Sprocket. Attach the remaining Spacer to the other Sprocket in the same manner as the first, so that the set screw hole faces the top of the Sprocket.

5. To assemble one pedal, insert a Pedal Pin into the hole near each end of one Pedal Frame, as shown in **Figure Z**. Insert the opposite ends of these Pins into the corresponding holes in a second Pedal Frame, as shown. Glue the Pins in place. Assemble an identical pedal in the same manner.

6. Now install one assembled pedal on the outside of one pedal sprocket, as shown in **Figure AA**. To do this, insert a Pedal Shaft into the off-center hole in one Sprocket, on the side without the Spacer, and glue in place. The Shaft should not extend beyond the Sprocket on the side with the Spacer. Cut a ½-inch-diameter center hole in one of the plastic washers, and slip the washer over the end of the Shaft. Guide the outer end of the Shaft through the aligned center holes of one assembled pedal, but do not use glue. Install a solid plastic washer on the outer end of the Shaft, using one of the sheet metal screws, as shown. The pedal should be able to rotate around the center Shaft fairly easily. Assemble the remaining pedal, pedal sprocket, and shaft in the same manner.

7. The next step is to install the pedal-and-sprocket assemblies on the axle that extends through the sprocket post. Slip a large metal washer over one end of the axle. Install one sprocket, spacer side first, over the same end of the axle, as shown in **Figure BB**. The axle end should be flush with the outside surface of the

Figure CC

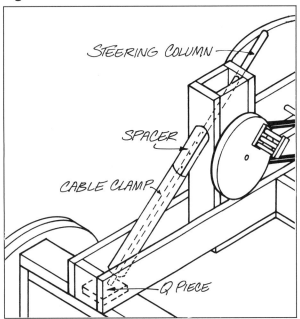

STEERING COLUMN

SPACER

CABLE CLAMP

Q PIECE

Figure DD

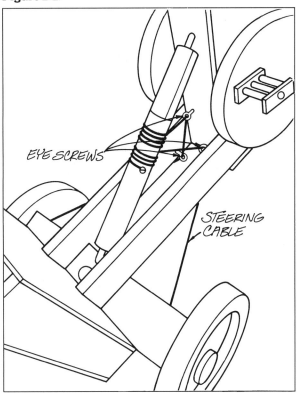

EYE SCREWS

STEERING CABLE

sprocket. To secure the sprocket assembly, rotate it until the hole that was drilled into the edge of the spacer is aligned with the hole near the end of the axle. Insert an 8d nail through the hole in the spacer and into the hole in the axle, as shown. Drive the nail on into the other side of the Spacer. Install the remaining sprocket assembly on the other end of the axle in the same manner, rotating it so that the pedals are at opposite points, as shown.

Assembling the Steering Mechanism

1. The assembled steering mechanism is shown in **Figure CC**. So that you won't get it all backwards to begin with, remember that the upper end of the 28½-inch steering column is the one that has been drilled ⅜ inch from the end. The lower end is the one that has been drilled 2½ inches from the end. To begin, insert the steering column down through the holes in the post, lower end first. Slip the Cable Clamp over the lower end of the steering column, and rotate it until the small holes in the Cable Clamp are aligned with the two lower holes in the steering column. Insert a screw into each hole to keep the steering column from turning inside the Cable Clamp.

2. Push the end of the steering column into the socket in the **Q** piece at the front of the frame, as shown in **Figure CC**. To install the two halves of the Steering Column Spacer, place them around the steering column between the post and the Cable Clamp, with the mitered end against the post, as shown. Nail the two halves of the Spacer together around the steering column as shown.

3. Two eyescrews will guide the steering cable to each end of the front axle support. For the cable that will run to the right-hand end of the axle support, install one eyescrew on the front of the post even with the upper edge of the frame, as shown in **Figure DD**. Install another eyescrew near the lower edge of the right-hand frame Rail, on the inside surface, 1½ inches from the post front, as shown. For the left-hand cable, install the upper eyescrew on the post front, 2 inches below the upper edge of the frame Rail, as shown. Install the lower left-hand eyescrew directly opposite the lower right-hand one, as shown.

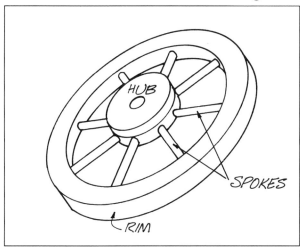

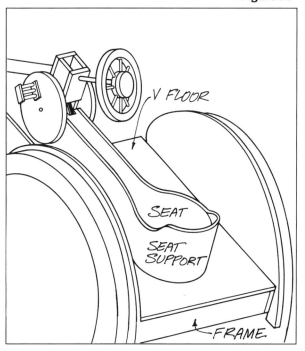

4. Install one eyescrew on the inside surface of each axle support R piece, ¾ inch from the back edge as shown in **Figure DD**.

5. Cut the plastic-covered cable in half, so that you have two 3-foot lengths. To attach one cable, tie one end to the eyescrew near the right-hand end of the axle support, as shown in **Figure DD**. Thread the cable up through the eyescrew guides on that side, as shown. Position the front wheels so that the tractor rolls straight forward. Wrap the cable clockwise around the Cable Clamp, starting near the top of the Clamp and working downward. Keep the cable taut as you work. Insert a flat washer over the end of a ¾-inch-long screw, and start the screw into the Cable Clamp near the end of the cable. Wrap the end of the cable around the screw, underneath the washer, and tighten the screw to secure the cable. Install the second cable in the same manner, beginning at the left-hand end of the axle support. Wrap it counterclockwise around the Clamp, working from just below the first screw downward.

6. To assemble the steering wheel, insert a Spoke through each hole in the T Steering Rim, and push it into a socket in the Steering Wheel Hub, as shown in **Figure EE**. Glue the spokes in place, and trim the ends of the spokes even with the outer edge of the rim. To install the steering wheel on the steering column, insert the upper end of the column into the center hole in the

hub. The steering wheel should be turned so that the hub extends out toward the driver. Adjust and rotate the steering wheel so that the set screw hole in the hub is aligned with the hole near the end of the column. Insert a screw through the aligned holes, and into the opposite side of the hub.

Assembling the Seat and Fenders

1. The assembled seat is shown in **Figure FF**. Note that the M Seat with the longer groove should be at the bottom, and the M Seat with the shorter groove should be at the top. To begin, bend the thin Seat Support around the curved edge of the lower Seat piece, using glue and escutcheon nails to secure the assembly as you go. The straight lower edge of the Seat Support should be flush with the bottom of the Seat piece, and all front edges should be even. Now place the upper Seat inside the curved Seat Support, and use glue and escutcheon nails to secure it. The upper edge of the Support should be flush with the top of the Seat at the front, but the Support will extend up above the Seat at the back, forming a backrest.

Figure GG

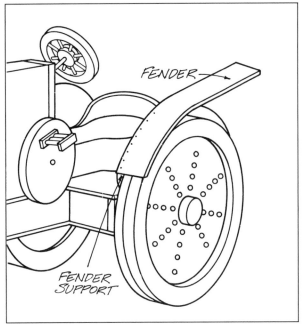

FENDER

FENDER
SUPPORT

Figure II

Y

NOTCH

FRAME

Figure HH

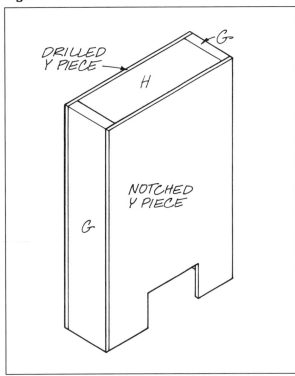

DRILLED
Y PIECE

H

G

NOTCHED
Y PIECE

G

2. To attach the assembled seat to the V Floor, align the long groove in the lower seat piece with the groove in the Floor so that the back ends of the grooves are even. The seat should extend 2½ inches beyond the front grooved edge of the Floor. Attach the seat to the Floor by inserting screws up through the Floor into the lower seat.

3. Install the floor-and-seat assembly on the rear portion of the frame, so that the rear edge of the floor is even with the rear end of the frame, as shown in **Figure FF**. Be sure that the V-belt does not bind on the floor or seat grooves. Attach the assembly to the frame using screws only, so that it can be removed if the belt wears out or comes off the pulleys.

4. To attach one Fender, place one end even with the lower edge of a Fender Support, as shown in **Figure GG**. Nail the Fender along the curved edge of the Support using escutcheon nails, and bending the Fender carefully along the curve. The Fender should extend out over the wheel, and the inner edge should be even with the inside surface of the Fender Support. Attach the remaining Fender to the opposite Support in the same manner.

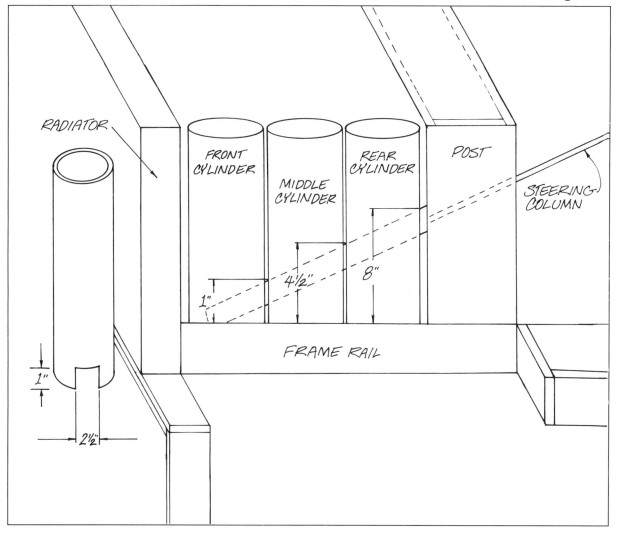

Assembling the Radiator, Engine Cylinders, and Hood

1. The assembled radiator is shown in **Figure HH**. To begin, attach a G piece to each end of the H piece, butting the edges as shown. Nail the notched Y piece over one side of this frame, and the drilled Y piece over the opposite side, as shown.

2. To install the radiator, slip the notch in the rear Y piece over the front end of the tractor frame, as shown in **Figure II**. Slide the radiator backward until the front end of the frame is butted against the inside surface of the drilled Y piece. Secure the radiator to the frame using glue and nails.

3. The engine Cylinders are lengths of PVC pipe, and are glued to the frame between the radiator and the steering/pedal post as shown in **Figure JJ**. Cut three 1-foot lengths of PVC pipe for the Cylinders. Each Cylinder must be notched to fit over the steering column. All of the notches are 2½ inches wide. For the Front Cylinder, cut a 1 x 2½-inch notch as shown in the detail diagram, **Figure JJ**. For the Middle Cylinder, first cut a 1

Figure KK

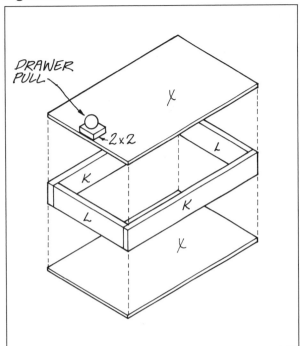

Figure LL

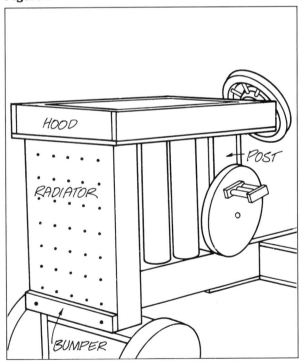

x 2½-inch notch, and then turn the pipe around and cut a 4½x 2½-inch notch directly opposite the first notch. For the Rear Cylinder, first cut a 4½ x 2½-inch notch, and then rotate the pipe and cut an 8 x 2½-inch notch directly opposite.

4. To install the Front Cylinder, place the lower notched end on top of the frame Rails so that the notch straddles the steering column, and glue in place as shown in **Figure JJ**. Attach the Middle and Rear Cylinders to the frame in the same manner, as shown.

5. The assembled hood is a simple box, and is shown in **Figure KK**. To begin, assemble a rectangular frame using the K and L pieces, butting the ends together as shown. The K pieces should cover the ends of the L pieces. Nail an **X** piece over one side of this frame. To create the hood ornament, use the 1-inch length of 2 x 2 and the spherical wooden drawer pull. Drill a screw hole through the center of the 2 x 2, and drill a matching screw socket up into the drawer pull if it does not already have one. Place the drilled 2 x 2 on top of the remaining **X** piece, centered between the long edges and flush with one end. Place the drawer pull on top, and insert a screw up through the **X** piece, through the 2 x 2, and into the drawer pull. This **X** piece will be attached to the hood assembly after you have installed the hood on the tractor.

6. Cut a 1½ x 12-inch Front Bumper from leftover 1-inch stock. Attach it to the front of the radiator, flush with the lower edge, as shown in **Figure LL**.

7. To install the hood, place the assembled portion over the radiator and steering/pedal post with the covered side down, as shown in **Figure LL**. Center the front end of the hood over the radiator, and align the back end even with the back edge of the steering/pedal post. Insert screws down through the floor of the hood into the radiator and post. Place the **X** hood top over the hood, with the ornament at the front end, and secure with screws. (If you prefer, you can attach the hood top to the hood at the back edge only, using a long piano hinge, and secure the front with a lunch-box catch. This way, the hood can be opened and used to store such important kiddie stuff as frogs, canned green slime, and melted candy bars.)